# Cappuccino with
# Colossians

Advancing the Ministries of the Gospel
**AMG** *Publishers*

*God's Word to you is our highest calling.*

## SANDRA GLAHN

Coffee Cup Bible Studies
*Cappuccino with Colossians*

© 2007 by Sandra L. Glahn

Published by AMG Publishers. All Rights Reserved.

Published in association with the literary
agency of Alive Communications, Inc., 7860 Goddard Street, Suite 200,
Colorado Springs, Colorado, 80920

No part of this publication, including the artwork, may be reproduced,
stored in a retrieval system, or transmitted in any form or by any means,
electronic, mechanical, photocopying, recording, or otherwise—except for
brief quotations in printed reviews, without the prior written permission
of the publisher.

Second Printing, 2008

ISBN 10: 0-89957-234-0
ISBN 13: 978-089957234-5

Unless otherwise noted, Scripture is taken from the NET Bible.
Copyright © 1996–2005 by Biblical Studies Press (www.bible.org). Used by
permission.

Scripture quotations marked (NASB) are from the New American Standard
Bible®. Copyright © 1960, 1962, 1963, 1968, 1971, 1972, 1973, 1975,
1977, 1995, by The Lockman Foundation. Used by permission.
(www.Lockman.org)

Scripture quotations marked (NIV) are from the Holy Bible, New
International Version, copyright 1973, 1978, 1984, International Bible
Society. Used by permission of Zondervan Publishing House

Editing and Proofreading: Diane Stortz and Rick Steele
Interior Design: PerfecType, Nashville, Tennessee
Cover Design: ImageWright Marketing and Design, Chattanooga, Tennessee

Printed in the United States of America
13 12 11 10 09 08 –CH– 7 6 5 4 3 2

# Acknowledgments

- Gary, my beloved husband, you embody *hesed*. Thank you for your loyal love, for believing in me before I believed in myself, and for cheering me on. Thanks, too, for designing and maintaining the Web site component of the Coffee Cup series. I'm grateful for your partnership in every way.

- Ken Mauger, Elliot Green, David Lowery, John Grassmick, and Dan Wallace—you labored to teach me Greek. I appreciate you.

- Gary Inrig, your messages in Colossians taught us that all truth is God's truth and all work done to the glory of God is ministry. Thank you.

- Women of Reinhardt Bible Church's Bible study, you first explored this book with me in my early days as a Bible teacher. I was young, but you listened anyway. I am especially indebted to Gladys Phillips and Nancy Moon, older women willing to teach the younger. Though they are now absent from the body and present with the Lord, their investment continues. Elizabeth Inrig, thank you for teaching me—and modeling for us all—that a mark of Christian maturity is giving away power.

- Members of Biblical Studies Press (www.bible.org) and translators of the NET Bible, apart from your essential ministry the *Coffee Cup Bible Studies* series would not even be possible. Thank you for laboring without compensation so others might grow in the Word. May God richly reward you in this life and the next.

- Chip MacGregor, my agent, thanks for representing me, for finding a home for this series, for your boundless encouragement, and your lacerating wit.

- Virginia Swint, thank you for thinking I rarely make mistakes, regardless of how much evidence you have to suggest otherwise. I appreciate your enthusiastic encouragement, your faithful prayers, and for always volunteering to edit. A friend loves at all times, and you have proven yourself a true friend.

- Dan Penwell of AMG, thank you for your generous encouragement and for championing the series.

- Rick Steele and Diane Stortz of AMG, I appreciate your good eyes and sharp editing scalpel that have saved me from my own typographical, language, and grammatical blunders time and again.

- Dr. Bill, you steered me to Colossians on a transatlantic flight as our team returned from our first Russia trip in the 1990s—guidance that has led to a lifelong love of the book. I'm grateful to and for you.

- David Johnson, you provided my first below-the-surface encounter with the text. Thank you for your years of faithful teaching and for your friendship.

- And finally, thanks to those who are praying that God will use His word through this series to change lives. You know who you are, and so does He. May He reward in public what you have done in secret.

# INTRODUCTION TO THE
## COFFEE CUP BIBLE STUDIES

"The precepts of the Lord are right, rejoicing the heart;
the commandment of the Lord is pure, enlightening the eyes."
(Psalm 19:8 NASB)

Congratulations! You have chosen wisely. By choosing to study the Bible, you have elected to spend time learning that which will rejoice the heart and enlighten the eyes.

And while any study in the Bible is time well spent, the *Coffee Cup Bible Studies* series has some unique elements that set it apart from others. So before we get started, let's talk about some of those elements designed to help you maximize your study time.

*Life rhythms.* Most participants in any Bible study have little problem keeping up during the week, when they have a routine, but on the weekends there's a general "falling off." Thus, *Coffee Cup Bible Studies* contain Monday-through-Friday Bible-study questions, but the Saturday and Sunday segments consist of short, more passive readings that draw application and insight from the texts you'll be considering. Know that the days listed here are mere suggestions. Some find it preferable to attend a Bible study one day and follow a four-day-per-week study schedule along with weekend readings. Feel free to change the structure of days and assignments to best fit your own needs.

*Community.* While the studies in the Coffee Cup series can be completed individually, they are also ideal for group interaction. If you don't have a local group with which to meet, find a few friends and start one. Or connect with others through www.soulpersuit.com, where you can participate, if you'd like, by engaging in artistic expressions as you interact with the text. These vehicles give you opportunities to share with a wider community what you're learning.

*Aesthetics.* At the author's Web site (www.aspire2.com) in a section designed for the Coffee Cup series, you will find links to art that depicts what's being discussed. You'll discover works such as Francesco Botticini's *The Assumption of the Virgin* (National Gallery London), which shows three hierarchies and nine orders of angels—based loosely on Colossians 1:16. Or look for listings of music CDs to help you memorize "psalms, hymns, and spiritual songs" (3:16). You'll also find links to other studies in Colossians and good commentaries and resource material. The more senses you can engage in your interaction with God's truth, the better you will remember it and the more you'll enjoy it.

*Convenience.* Rather than turning in the Bible to find the references, you'll find the entire text for each day included in this Coffee Cup study book (thanks to the Biblical Studies Foundation). While it's important to know our way around the Bible, the Coffee Cup series is designed this way so you can take the book with you and study the Bible on the subway, at a coffee shop, in a doctors' waiting room, or on your lunch break. The chosen translation is the NET Bible, which is accessible online from virtually anywhere in the world. The owners of this translation have graciously granted me the most generous copyright freedoms of any contemporary translation, making it possible for readers to have the biblical text itself in their books.

The NET Bible is a modern translation from the ancient Greek, Hebrew, and Aramaic texts. Both the online and text versions of the NET Bible include 60,932 translators' notes and citations pulling from more than 700 scholarly works. You can learn more about the NET Bible, along with numerous textual notes, at www.bible.org, which serves 3.5 million people worldwide.

*Sensitivity to time-and-culture considerations.* Many Bible studies skip what we call the theological step; that is, they go straight from observing and interpreting the words given to those in a different time and culture to applying those words in a modern-day setting. The result is sometimes misapplication (such as "Paul told slaves to obey their masters, so we need to obey our employers"). In the Coffee Cup series, our aim is to be particularly sensitive to the audience to whom the "mail" was addressed. We work to take the crucial step of separating what was intended for a limited audience from what is for all audiences for all time (love God; love your neighbor).

*Sensitivity to genres.* Rather than crafting a series in which each study is laid out exactly like all the others, each Coffee Cup study is structured to best present the genre being examined—whether epistle, poetry, gospel, history, or narrative. The way we study Colossians (an epistle, or letter) differs from how someone might study the compact poetry in Song of Songs. So while the studies in the Coffee Cup series may have similar elements, no two will take quite the same approach.

# INTRODUCTION TO
# CAPPUCCINO WITH COLOSSIANS

Have you ever loved someone you've never met? A father sent on military assignment shortly before his child's birth surely loves that child he's never seen. One of my friends met her husband in an online chat room. They loved each other long before they met. And Peter wrote to Christ-followers about Jesus, "You have not seen him, but you love him" (1 Peter 1:8). If you know the Lord, the one you love more than any other is someone you've never seen.

Imagine you're a Christian in Colossae. Your city, one of several in Phyrgia, sits on a rocky ridge above the Lycus River, a branch of the Maeander. Three miles away stands Mt. Cadmus, elevation eight thousand feet. People pass through Colossae on their way from Ephesus to the Euphrates. Ephesus is about one hundred miles west and boasts one of the Seven Wonders of the World, the Temple of Artemis.

Much closer, at eleven miles, lies Laodicea, and thirteen miles away is Hierapolis. Six centuries earlier, during the Persian wars (see text boxes), your city was well-known, but as its companion cities Laodicea and Hierapolis have grown, Colossae has declined.[1] Now yours is a second-rate market town, thanks to a rerouting of the highway through Laodicea. Still, Colossae continues as a trade-route stop on the way east, thanks to its sheep and their unusual purplish wool.

---

[1] Robert Gromacki, *Philippians and Colossians* (Chattanooga: AMG Publishers, 2003), 122.

It's the year AD 60. You live during Nero's reign—not the safest time and place for those who believe in Jesus as Lord—and you serve as a citizen of the Roman Empire. You gather regularly with other believers, most of them Gentile rather than Jewish, in the home of a man named Philemon. And most of those believers have never actually met the apostle Paul.

Who is Paul? Initially called Saul, he was a native of Tarsus and of pure Jewish descent. You know nothing of his mother, and all you know about his father is that he was a Pharisee (Acts 23:6). From his father, Saul received his Roman citizenship (22:28). Of the tribe of Benjamin (Phil. 3:5), it has been said Saul was born in the second year after the birth of Jesus.[2] Sometime around age thirteen, he went to Jerusalem to study under Gamaliel, a distinguished Jewish teacher (Acts 22:3).

Now known as Paul, the apostle is a tentmaker by trade, but as a Roman citizen he is in the aristocracy of any provisional town. Besides being a citizen, he is a Tarsian (Tarsus being a decent place to hail from), a Hebrew, and a Pharisee. At one time he had a reputation for hating Christians; he stood by as a bloodthirsty crowd in Jerusalem made Stephen a martyr and in a zealous blaze, the Pharisee pursued those who believed in Jesus as Christ (Acts 7–8). Yet God miraculously appeared to him, and he became a Christian.

Following his conversion, Paul preached Christ in the synagogues and lived Christ in the streets, gaining him a reputation as a giant in the Christian faith. The churches now number him among the apostles. After beginning to take the good news to the Gentiles, he has faced great danger from the Jews and has been arrested and punished numerous times.

Though Paul has never visited your city, you love and respect him. And your friends Philemon (Philem. 1:1) and Epaphras (Col. 4:12),

---

*481 BC. Xerxes [probably the king who would later take Esther as his queen] . . . pressed forward upon his march; and passing Anaua, a Phrygian city, and a lake from which salt is gathered, he came to Colossae, a Phrygian city of great size, situated at a spot where the river Lycus plunges into a chasm and disappears. This river, after running under ground a distance of about five furlongs, reappears once more, and empties itself, like the stream above mentioned, into the Maeander.—Herodotus, The Histories, vii.30, written 440 BC*

---

[2] *Unger's Bible Dictionary*, 831.

men of Colossae, know him well. About six years earlier, Paul began a three-year residency in nearby Ephesus (see Acts 20:31), where he met Philemon and Epaphras. Epaphras came to faith through Paul's witness, and once Epaphras grew in the faith, he returned to Colossae to share the gospel. You heard about Jesus from him (see Col. 1:7).

Paul calls Philemon a "colaborer" (Philem. 1:1) known for his hospitality (5–7).[3] You also know Philemon's family—Apphia, his wife (1:2), and Archippus, Paul's "fellow soldier" (1:2), whom, Paul describes as having a "ministry in the Lord" (a phrase many take as a reference to church office) (Col. 4:17).

One day when you were meeting with God's people for worship, you heard some commotion at the door. There stood Philemon's runaway slave, Onesimus—unbound. By law, a master has the right to punish such a runaway slave with death, and up to that point you had

> Cyrus [the Younger, in 401 BC] with the troops which I have named, set out from Sardis, and marched on and on through Lydia three stages, making two-and-twenty parasangs, to the river Maeander. That river is two hundred feet broad, and was spanned by a bridge consisting of seven boats. Crossing it, he marched through Phrygia a single stage, of eight parasangs, to Colossae, an inhabited [probably meaning "populous," but could contrast with uninhabited, which many cities in Asia were at the time] city, prosperous and large. Here he remained seven days. . . . From this place he marched three stages, twenty parasangs in all, to Celaenae, a populous city of Phrygia, large and prosperous. Here Cyrus owned a palace and a large paradise full of wild beasts, which he used to hunt on horseback, whenever he wished to give himself or his horses exercise. Through the midst of the park flows the river Maeander, the sources of which are within the palace buildings.—Xenophon (c. 431–355 BC), Anabasis, i.2, 5–6

never heard of a runaway slave returning to his master of his own free will! And if that weren't enough of a shock, standing there with Onesimus was Tychicus of Asia, the apostle Paul's beloved friend and fellow servant. On top of that, Onesimus professed that he believed in Jesus Christ! He told how he had just come from seeing Paul in Rome

---

[3] According to tradition, Philemon was actually bishop of Colossae (*Apostolical Constitutions*, vii, 46), and the *Greek Martyrology* (Menae) for November 22 tells us that, together with his wife and son and Onesimus, he was martyred by stoning before Androcles, the governor, in the days of Nero. With this the Latin Martyrology agrees (compare Lightfoot, Ignatius, II, 535). *ISBE*, "Philemon."

and brought a full report of the apostle's prison ministry. You might not have believed it all except that Tychicus verified the whole story.

Onesimus and Tychicus had with them three letters from Paul. One was a personal missive to Philemon, asking him to forgive his rebel slave; another was addressed to the entire church in Colossae; and the third was intended for the believers in Ephesus (or perhaps Laodicea or even believers in a group of nearby cities).

Onesimus brought everyone up-to-date on Paul's comings and goings. After Paul's time in Ephesus, he was imprisoned for his faith and sent to Rome to await trial before Emperor Nero (Acts 25), to whom he appealed in the summer of AD 58. Epaphras traveled to Rome, where he found Paul imprisoned in rented quarters as he awaited trial.

About that time, Onesimus also had found Paul. Once Onesimus decided to return and make things right with Philemon, Paul, with the help of an *amanuensis* [pronounced uh-man-yoo-EN-sis], a writing secretary, composed the letters that Onesimus now delivered, and Paul sent Tychicus to accompany him.

In the letter to the church at Colossae, Paul refers to Epaphras as a "fellow prisoner" (Philem. 1:23). As they spent time together, Paul heard Epaphras pray and talk about you and the rest of his beloved Colossian fellow believers who struggle to cling to the truth amidst heresy.

Fast forward two thousand years. As we consider these events that happened long ago, we have some pieces of information that we try to fit together like a 3-D puzzle. First, we know an earthquake hit Colossae in AD 60, probably the same year Paul wrote. He does not mention it in his letter, so it may have happened shortly after he wrote to the Colossians, or perhaps the news had not reached him yet.

Paul also doesn't mention exactly what heresy (or heresies) the Colossian believers faced, but we can get a general idea from the concerns he addresses. Looking together at the books of Colossians, Ephesians, and Philemon, we can find numerous clues. Here's our best guess: Some in the congregation were into angel worship. Others argued that God could not have created the world because, they said, matter is evil. Others found mystery religions fascinating; some emphasized spiritual techniques for getting in touch with spiritual beings. And some may have falsely taught that believers had to have a certain level of secret knowledge or spirituality to hear from God. Because of the city's location on the way to the East, there were Eastern and occult influences in Colossians during this time as well.

To add to the Colossians' difficulties, Jewish believers, with their ancient traditions, wanted to do things "the way we have always done it." Possibly they insisted that, to please God, Gentile believers had to keep the Law. If you were a grown man who had recently trusted Christ, would you want to be circumcised in order to continue growing in the faith?

You'll notice, though, what Paul doesn't do in response to the Colossians' challenges: He doesn't list topics such as how to exorcise demons or how to pray for one another or even how to integrate Jewish and Gentile believers. He avoids teaching a system to refute wrong ideas. Instead he presents a person, one available not just to a gifted few but to all—the Lord Jesus Christ, supreme and sufficient.

Colossians is full of timeless truth. Many churches today create programs in the name of being relevant. Yet consider the irony that the most relevant messages answer these age-old questions: Who is the Father? Who is the Son? Who is the Holy Spirit?

If you've read the news lately, if you've followed what's hot in the world of book publishing or movies or newspaper headlines, you know that the old Colossian problems keep showing up as many today try to refashion Jesus. Some say He didn't take on human flesh, that He was only a spirit. It's an old lie repackaged, developed more fully by the Gnostics late in the second century and served as leftovers in our time.

Today the ancient city of Colossae lies buried under an unexcavated hill in Turkey. The city was already in decline when Paul wrote to the people there, yet his words endure. The book of Colossians helps us think rightly about the second person of the Godhead, the Lord Jesus, the firstborn of all creation. Like the Colossians, we live in a time when people still ask, Who is Jesus? They reject the satisfying feast of the ancient faith in favor of reheated Gnostic thinking. And they think pluralistically, considering all religions equally valid (though they often call Christianity the one invalid view).

A great issue for the Colossians then and for us now is this: Who is Jesus Christ and what are the ramifications of that? Is he a god? A created power? Or is he exalted Lord and Master?

What we think about God and what He thinks about us are the most important things about us.

# CONTENTS

# WEEK 1 OF 4

## *Christ the Firstborn: Colossians 1:1–23*

**"It's amazing—not that I walked on the moon, but that He walked on earth."—Neil Armstrong**

## SUNDAY: WHOM HAVING NOT SEEN YOU LOVE

**Scripture:** "You learned the gospel from Epaphras, our dear fellow slave—a faithful minister of Christ on our behalf—who also told us of your love in the Spirit. For this reason we also, from the day we heard about you, have not ceased praying for you and asking God to fill you with the knowledge of his will in all spiritual wisdom and understanding." (Col. 1:7–9)

Lucy Vorobyova was an English teacher in Belarus. On our first day in Minsk, her city, my husband and I ate lunch with Lucy and her husband, Sergei. We instantly enjoyed their humor, their kind words, and their encouraging sentiments. Starting on the second day, Lucy worked as my translator, pressing on with a zeal that kept me going when I felt too exhausted to continue.

The year was 1994. We had come to Minsk to talk about our faith and hand out free Bibles to anyone interested, making ourselves available in flats and parks and public schools. After decades of Communism and religious persecution, the landscape had changed. People came in droves to receive free copies of Scripture and to hear about the good news that had been in the former USSR a thousand years before it came to America, but which Communists had suppressed for the past seventy.

While Lucy did not believe initially, she marveled at the response of her comrades and loved that we were returning to her culture something the Communists had taken away. That thought sometimes drove her with more passion than I had. "Sandi!" she would insist, "we have time to tell one more person before lunch. Come on!"

She translated for me when avowed atheists conversed about their doubts and ended up professing faith in Christ on the spot. She gained so much proficiency at answering their questions that sometimes she didn't even bother to translate—she knew what our answers would be. (It's not like the questions were difficult. People asked things like "Is Jesus as old as George Bush?" and "Is Jesus dead or still alive?")

One evening on the way back to our central meeting place, I asked Lucy, "What is keeping you from believing?"

She stopped on the sidewalk and stared at her feet, deep in thought. Finally she looked up at me and smiled. "Sandi . . . I think . . . nothing!" She knew what to do—she had shared it already so many times. Right there on that sidewalk she prayed, expressing her belief. Afterward, the hugs and tears flowed. That night she learned that Sergei had also trusted Christ that day.

How we loved that young couple and their enthusiasm! By the end of the week, we wept bitterly when the time came for us to depart.

Once my husband and I returned to the states, vast expanses of land and sea separated us. We had limited internet access; they had none. Mail service proved undependable. No Bible teaching church existed where they could go to learn more about their newfound faith. So we needed to return. Compelled by a deep longing to assure ourselves of their welfare, we went back with a medical team eight months later. We had to know how they were!

Of course we took as many resources as we could fit in our bags. Among them were some items from my friend Peggy—two Christian books, vitamins for their children, and a letter of greeting that included verses about God's character. Peggy had heard of Lucy and Sergei so often through our prayers and stories that she had grown to love and care for these people she had never met.

And I saw in Peggy's actions some similarities to Paul's relationship with the Colossian Christians. Though he had never met them, his friend Epaphras loved the Colossians with whom he had shared the gospel. Paul, along with his friend Timothy, prayed with Epaphras for the Colossian believers, knowing they lived in a culture filled with false doctrine. And when two of their friends set out from Rome for Colossae, Paul wrote the believers there a letter intended to help them understand this Jesus in whom they had believed.

Here's how he began: "From Paul, an apostle of Christ Jesus by the will of God, and Timothy our brother, to the saints, the faithful brothers and sisters in Christ, at Colossae. Grace and peace to you from God our Father! We always give thanks to God, the Father of our Lord Jesus Christ, when we pray for you, since we heard about your faith in Christ Jesus and the love that you have for all the saints. Your faith and love have arisen from the hope laid up for you in heaven, which you have heard about in the message of truth, the gospel that has come to you. Just as in the entire world this gospel is bearing fruit" (Col. 1:1–6).

Upon our return to Minsk, we found Lucy and Sergei reading their Bibles daily, their texts filled with underlined verses. They lacked the fellowship of other Christ-followers, yet they were growing in their faith. Still, they had many questions. Unprotected against cults, they needed more grounding in their understanding of the person and work of Jesus Christ, the authority of Scripture, and other important doctrines. So our top priority was to help them understand the faith they had so willingly embraced.

Paul didn't have the luxury of actually meeting the Colossian believers. Yet he knew their greatest need, greater even than physical safety, and it was the same need we found evident in Lucy and Sergei. It's our need to know everything we can about Jesus Christ. We need to know that He is not just a man, nor is He lacking in humanity. He created all things; He is before all things; in Him all things hold together. He is the image of the invisible God!

## MONDAY: THE LETTER

1. Ask for God's Spirit to give you wisdom, insight, and illumination; then read the entire letter to the Colossians in one sitting. It's shorter than a magazine article.

## Salutation

### Colossians 1

**1:1** From Paul, an apostle of Christ Jesus by the will of God, and Timothy our brother, **1:2** to the saints, the faithful brothers and sisters in Christ, at Colossae. Grace and peace to you from God our Father!

### Paul's Thanksgiving and Prayer for the Church

**1:3** We always give thanks to God, the Father of our Lord Jesus Christ, when we pray for you, **1:4** since we heard about your faith in Christ Jesus and the love that you have for all the saints. **1:5** Your faith and love have arisen from the hope laid up for you in heaven, which you have heard about in the message of truth, the gospel **1:6** that has come to you. Just as in the entire world this gospel is bearing fruit and growing, so it has also been bearing fruit and growing among you from the first day you heard it and understood the grace of God in truth. **1:7** You learned the gospel from Epaphras, our dear fellow slave—a faithful minister of Christ on our behalf—**1:8** who also told us of your love in the Spirit.

### Paul's Prayer for the Growth of the Church

**1:9** For this reason we also, from the day we heard about you have not ceased praying for you and asking God to fill you with the knowledge of his will in all spiritual wisdom and understanding, **1:10** so that you may live worthily of the Lord and please him in all respects—bearing fruit in every good deed, growing in the knowledge of God, **1:11** being strengthened with all power according to his glorious might for the display of all patience and steadfastness, joyfully **1:12** giving thanks to the Father who has qualified you to share in the saints' inheritance in the light. **1:13** He delivered us from the power of darkness and transferred us to the kingdom of the Son he loves, 1:14 in whom we have redemption, the forgiveness of sins.

### The Supremacy of Christ

**1:15** He is the image of the invisible God, the firstborn over all creation,

**1:16** for all things in heaven and on earth were created by him—all things, whether visible or invisible, whether thrones or dominions, whether principalities or powers—all things were created through him and for him.

**1:17** He himself is before all things and all things are held together in him.

**1:18** He is the head of the body, the church, as well as the beginning, the firstborn from among the dead, so that he himself may become first in all things.

**1:19** For God was pleased to have all his fullness dwell in the Son

**1:20** and through him to reconcile all things to himself by making peace through the blood of his cross—through him, whether things on earth or things in heaven.

### Paul's Goal in Ministry

**1:21** And you were at one time strangers and enemies in your minds as expressed through your evil deeds, **1:22** but now he has reconciled you by his physical body through death to present you holy, without blemish, and blameless before him—**1:23** if indeed you remain in the faith, established and firm, without shifting from the hope of the gospel that you heard. This gospel has also been preached in all creation under heaven, and I, Paul, have become its servant.

**1:24** Now I rejoice in my sufferings for you, and I fill up in my physical body—for the sake of his body, the church—what is lacking in the sufferings of Christ. **1:25** I became a servant of the church according to the stewardship from God—given to me for you—in order to complete the word of God, **1:26** that is, the mystery that has been kept hidden from ages and generations, but has now been revealed to his saints. **1:27** God wanted to make known to them the glorious riches of this mystery among the Gentiles, which is Christ in you, the hope of glory. **1:28** We proclaim him by instructing and teaching all people with all wisdom so that we may present every person mature in Christ. **1:29** Toward this goal I also labor, struggling according to his power that powerfully works in me.

### Colossians 2

**2:1** For I want you to know how great a struggle I have for you, and for those in Laodicea, and for those who have not met me face to face. **2:2** My goal is that their hearts, having been knit together in love, may be encouraged, and that they may have all the riches that assurance brings in their understanding of the knowledge of the mystery of God, namely, Christ, **2:3** in whom are hidden all the treasures of wisdom and knowledge. **2:4** I say this so that no one will deceive you through arguments that sound reasonable. **2:5** For though I am absent from you in body, I am present with you in spirit, rejoicing to see your morale and the firmness of your faith in Christ.

**2:6** Therefore, just as you received Christ Jesus as Lord, continue to live your lives in him, **2:7** rooted and built up in him and firm in your faith just as you were taught, and overflowing with thankfulness. **2:8** Be careful not to allow anyone to captivate you through an empty, deceitful philosophy that is according to human traditions and the elemental spirits of the world, and not according to Christ. **2:9** For in him all the fullness of deity lives in bodily form, **2:10** and you have been filled in him, who is the head over every ruler and authority. **2:11** In him you also were circumcised—not, however, with a circumcision performed by human hands, but by the removal of the fleshly body, that is, through the circumcision done by Christ. **2:12** Having been buried with him in baptism, you also have been raised with him through your faith in the power of God who raised him from the dead. **2:13** And even though you were dead in your transgressions and in the uncircumcision of your flesh, he nevertheless made you alive with him, having forgiven all your transgressions. **2:14** He has destroyed what was against us, a certificate of indebtedness expressed in decrees opposed to us. He has taken it away by nailing it to the cross. **2:15** Disarming the rulers and authorities, he has made a public disgrace of them, triumphing over them by the cross.

**2:16** Therefore do not let anyone judge you with respect to food or drink, or in the matter of a feast, new moon, or Sabbath days—**2:17** these are only the shadow of the things to come, but the reality is Christ! **2:18** Let no one who delights in humility and the worship of angels pass judgment on you. That person goes on at great lengths about what he has supposedly seen, but he is puffed up with empty notions by his fleshly mind. **2:19** He has not held fast to the head from whom the whole body, supported and knit together through its ligaments and sinews, grows with a growth that is from God.

**2:20** If you have died with Christ to the elemental spirits of the world, why do you submit to them as though you lived in the world? **2:21** "Do not handle! Do not taste! Do not touch!" **2:22** These are all destined to perish with use, founded as they are on human commands and teachings. **2:23** Even though they have the appearance of wisdom with their self-imposed worship and false humility achieved by an unsparing treatment of the body—a wisdom with no true value—they in reality result in fleshly indulgence.

## Colossians 3

**3:1** Therefore, if you have been raised with Christ, keep seeking the things above, where Christ is, seated at the right hand of God. **3:2** Keep thinking about things above, not things on the earth, **3:3** for you have died and your life is hidden with Christ in God. **3:4** When Christ (who is your life) appears, then you too will be revealed in glory with him. **3:5** So put to death whatever in your nature belongs to the earth: sexual immorality, impurity, shameful passion, evil desire, and greed which is idolatry. **3:6** Because of these things the wrath of God is coming on the sons of disobedience. **3:7** You also lived your lives in this way at one time, when you used to live among them. **3:8** But now, put off all such things as anger, rage, malice, slander, abusive language from your mouth. **3:9** Do not lie to one another since you have put off the old man with its practices **3:10** and have been clothed with the new man that is being renewed in knowledge according to the image of the one who created it. **3:11** Here there is neither Greek nor Jew, circumcised or uncircumcised, barbarian, Scythian, slave or free, but Christ is all and in all.

**3:12** Therefore, as the elect of God, holy and dearly loved, clothe yourselves with a heart of mercy, kindness, humility, gentleness, and patience, **3:13** bearing with one another and forgiving one another, if someone happens to have a complaint against anyone else. Just as the Lord has forgiven you, so you also forgive others. **3:14** And to all these virtues add love, which is the perfect bond. **3:15** Let the peace of Christ be in control in your heart (for you were in fact called as one body to this peace), and be thankful. **3:16** Let the word of Christ dwell in you richly, teaching and exhorting one another with all wisdom, singing psalms, hymns, and spiritual songs, all with grace in your hearts to God. **3:17** And whatever you do in word or deed, do it all in the name of the Lord Jesus, giving thanks to God the Father through him.

**3:18** Wives, submit to your husbands, as is fitting in the Lord. **3:19** Husbands, love your wives and do not be embittered against them. **3:20** Children, obey your parents in everything, for this is pleasing in the Lord. **3:21** Fathers, do not provoke your children, so they will not become disheartened. **3:22** Slaves, obey your earthly masters in every respect, not only when they are watching—like those who are strictly people-pleasers—but with a sincere heart, fearing the Lord. **3:23** Whatever you are doing, work at it with enthusiasm, as to the Lord and not for people, **3:24** because you know that you will receive your inheritance from the Lord as the reward. Serve the Lord Christ. **3:25** For the one who does wrong will be repaid for his wrong, and there are no exceptions.

### Colossians 4

**4:1** Masters, treat your slaves with justice and fairness, because you know that you also have a master in heaven. **4:2** Be devoted to prayer, keeping alert in it with thanksgiving. **4:3** At the same time pray for us too, that God may open a door for the message so that we may proclaim the mystery of Christ, for which I am in chains. **4:4** Pray that I may make it known as I should. 4:5 Conduct yourselves with wisdom toward outsiders, making the most of the opportunities. 4:6 Let your speech always be gracious, seasoned with salt, so that you may know how you should answer everyone.

**4:7** Tychicus, a dear brother, faithful minister, and fellow slave in the Lord, will tell you all the news about me. **4:8** I sent him to you for this very purpose, that you may know how we are doing and that he may encourage your hearts. **4:9** I sent him with Onesimus, the faithful and dear brother, who is one of you. They will tell you about everything here.

**4:10** Aristarchus, my fellow prisoner, sends you greetings, as does Mark, the cousin of Barnabas (about whom you received instructions; if he comes to you, welcome him). **4:11** And Jesus who is called Justus also sends greetings. In terms of Jewish converts, these are the only fellow workers for the kingdom of God, and they have been a comfort to me. **4:12** Epaphras, who is one of you and a slave of Christ, greets you. He is always struggling in prayer on your behalf, so that you may stand mature and fully assured in all the will of God. **4:13** For I can testify that he has worked hard for you and for those in Laodicea and Hierapolis. **4:14** Our dear friend Luke the physician and Demas greet you. **4:15** Give my greetings to the brothers and sisters who are in Laodicea and to Nympha and the church that meets in her house. **4:16** And after you have read this letter, have it read to the church of Laodicea. In turn, read the letter from Laodicea as well. **4:17** And tell Archippus, "See to it that you complete the ministry you received in the Lord." **4:18** I, Paul, write this greeting by my own hand. Remember my chains. Grace be with you.

2. What stood out to you or made you think as you read?

_____

_____

_____

3. Paul wrote under the inspiration of the Holy Spirit, penning God's Word for the Colossians and secondarily for us. What in your life needs to change immediately in response to God's Word?

_____

_____

_____

## TUESDAY: SALUTATIONS

1. Prayerfully read Colossians 1:1–4, which will be the first half of our focus for the day.

> **Colossians 1:1** From Paul, an apostle of Christ Jesus by the will of God, and Timothy our brother, **1:2** to the saints, the faithful brothers and sisters in Christ, at Colossae. Grace and peace to you from God our Father! **1:3** We always give thanks to God, the Father of our Lord Jesus Christ, when we pray for you, **1:4** since we heard about your faith in Christ Jesus and the love that you have for all the saints.

2. Who is writing the letter (1:1)?

_____

_____

• *An apostle.* In the strictest sense, an apostle was one of the twelve chosen by Jesus specifically to be sent out by Him. The word *apostle* comes from the Greek *apostolos*, meaning "sent one." The original twelve apostles included Judas. When he died, Matthias replaced him. In Acts 1:21–22 we read the qualifications of an apostle according to Peter: "Of the men who have accompanied us all the time that the Lord Jesus went in and out among us—beginning with the baptism of John, until the day that He was taken up from us—one of these must become a witness with us of His resurrection" (NASB).

Though Paul did not accompany the Lord nor see Jesus before the resurrection, he encountered Jesus post-resurrection on the road to Damascus and was called to be an apostle to the Gentiles. In his letters, when Paul greets his readers, he usually reminds them of his apostleship (see the first verses of Rom., 1 Cor., 2 Cor., Eph., 1 Tim., etc.), and Colossians is no exception.

Sometimes the title of apostle includes more than the twelve plus Paul. It's possible that the spiritual gift of apostle (see Eph. 4:11) is the equivalent to what we might call those we send to begin ministries—missionaries and church planters. Many translators believe Andronicus and Junia were known as being "among the apostles." One of the church fathers, John Chrysostom, wrote of Junia, "O how great is the devotion of this woman that she should be counted worthy of the appellation of apostle!" The early church called Mary Magdalene an apostle to the apostles because she announced to the twelve that Jesus was alive. This does not mean that she held the apostolic office; rather, she was given such a title because she was "sent" with the good news.

Most commonly, though, in the New Testament the word *apostle* is reserved for the twelve apostles to the Jews and for Paul, the apostle to the Gentiles. *Apostle* does not mean a mere messenger delivery service; rather, to be an apostle is to be an authoritative messenger of God. Since the Colossian believers did not personally know Paul, he used his title to remind them that he spoke by command of Christ.

3. To whom is the letter being written (1:2)?

_____

• *Saints.* When we hear the word *saint*, many of us think of a famous person known for being superspiritual and given this special title, such as St. Patrick or St. Valentine or St. Joan of Arc. Yet *saint* is a word the New Testament writers use to refer in general to all who have believed in Christ. The word means simply "set-apart ones."

Saints are not perfect, but they live holy lives, having been declared righteous by the work of Christ. Think of your friends in Christ. Each of them, according to Paul's usage, is a saint. Think of it—saint Mary, saint Jim, saint Bob, saint Jack. In my family it's saint Gary and saint Alexandra. What about you?

• *The faithful brothers and sisters in Christ.* Have you ever been to the city of Philadelphia—the city of brotherly love? The word for *brothers* Paul uses here has one of the same root words as we find in that city's name: *adelphos.* While the Greek word means "brothers," the NET Bible translators rendered it in English as "brothers and sisters" or "fellow Christians." That's because *brothers* in Greek is a lot like *amigos,* "friends," in Spanish; both its masculine and common (mixed company) endings are the same. *Amigos* are either all males or males and females. *Amigas* are women only. In the same way, *brothers* in Greek can mean either all males or males and females. Context tells us which. Paul is writing to both men and women in Colossae, and he uses the warm, familial sibling word that reminds them that all Christians have the same Father and so belong to the same family. That's why it is sometimes said that "Spirit is thicker than blood."

4. In the best of family relationships, how do brothers and sisters relate to each other?

_____

_____

_____

_____

Paul wrote to the church, the believers in Christ, in the city of Colossae about two thousand years ago, yet most of what he wrote is of benefit to believers today. While we may not live in a culture that accepts slavery as theirs did (see Col. 3:22), we can take what is timeless from the text and apply it to our time. And we certainly need, as they did, to know who Jesus is and how to "live worthily."

• *Grace.* The normal Greek salutation meant "greetings" or "favor from me to you." Yet Paul chose a different but related word, *charis*, "grace," which refers to God's unmerited favor bestowed on sinful individuals with no strings attached. Paul's greeting is a blessing, then, like a prayer that the lives of the believers in Colossae will be filled with God's unmerited favor.

5. List some ways in which you have been a recipient of God's grace.

_____

_____

_____

_____

6. Why does Paul give thanks for the Colossians (1:3–4)?

_____

_____

_____

7. Pray for insight and then read Colossians 1:5–8. Circle the word *gospel* each time it occurs.

> **1:5** Your faith and love have arisen from the hope laid up for you in heaven, which you have heard about in the message of truth, the gospel **1:6** that has come to you. Just as in the entire world this gospel is bearing fruit and growing, so it has also been bearing fruit and growing among you from the first day you heard it and understood the grace of God in truth. **1:7** You learned the gospel from Epaphras, our dear fellow slave—a faithful minister of Christ on our behalf—**1:8** who also told us of your love in the Spirit.

• *The message of truth, the gospel.* In 1 Corinthians 15, Paul seems to give a two-fold outline of what the gospel is—the death of Jesus (with the burial as evidence) and the resurrection of Jesus (with His appearances to eyewitnesses as evidence). It also includes the ramifications of these events.

1. Read today's section of Scripture focusing on Paul's prayer priorities.

> **Colossians 1:9** For this reason we also, from the day we heard about you, have not ceased praying for you and asking God to fill you with the knowledge of his will in all spiritual wisdom and understanding, **1:10** so that you may live worthily of the Lord and please him in all respects—bearing fruit in every good deed, growing in the knowledge of God, **1:11** being strengthened with all power according to his glorious might for the display of all patience and steadfastness, joyfully **1:12** giving thanks to the Father who has qualified you to share in the saints' inheritance in the light.

2. How regularly does Paul pray for these people he's never met (1:9)? How does your own perseverance in prayer compare with his?

_____

_____

_____

3. Why do you think Paul prays for the Colossians' knowledge of God's will to be accompanied by "spiritual wisdom and understanding"? What are some dangers of accumulating knowledge without such wisdom and understanding?

_____

_____

_____

4. What is the goal of this knowledge, wisdom, and understanding (1:10)?

_____

_____

5. In verse 10 Paul tells his readers how to live: worthily. The word translated *live* has the same root as words translated *walk* or *behave*. It's the way we conduct our lives. Paul prays that the Colossians would live worthily of the Lord and please Him in all respects. Do you think it's even possible to live in a way that's worthy of the sacrifice of Jesus? Why or why not?

_____

_____

_____

6. Paul provides some indications of what a worthy-walking life looks like. Notice how the ideas of "living worthily" and being "qualified" sit like bookends on either side of his description. Fill in the blanks:

- So that you may _____ of the Lord (1:10)
- Bearing _____ in every deed (1:10)
- Growing in the _____ (1:10)
- Being strengthened with all _____ (1:11)
- According to _____ (1:11)
- For the display _____ (1:11)
- Giving _____ to the Father (1:12)
- Who has _____ you to share in the saints' inheritance in the light (1:12)

7. Rather than seeing a life lived worthily as an unreachable standard, consider the potential God has given us for full living! By His grace and help, we can do so. What is the source of strengthening for living worthily (1:11)?

_____

_____

Have you ever attended a prayer meeting where the only requests were for physical healing? As someone who's had two surgeries requiring four major incisions in the last year, I deeply appreciate such prayers. Yet sometimes our requests include only needs in the material world to the exclusion of what's eternal. Notice Paul's priorities. He lives in an empire where Nero despises Christians. The apostle's movements are limited because he is imprisoned awaiting trial. Yet what is the focus of his prayers? His own deliverance? A hot meal? No! When he prays for the Colossians, his primary concern is something other than freedom and health; it is for their spiritual vitality. He wants the Colossian Christians to prosper, but look at the kind of prosperity he has in mind:

• Being filled with the knowledge of His will in all spiritual wisdom and understanding
  • Living worthily of the Lord and pleasing Him in all respects
  • Bearing fruit in every good deed
  • Growing in the knowledge of God
• Being strengthened with all power according to His glorious might for the display of all patience and steadfastness, joyfully
  • Giving thanks to the Father who has qualified you to share in the saints' inheritance in the light

8. Pray through this list from Colossians 1:10–12 for yourself, asking God to make your life look the way Paul wants the Colossian believers' lives to look. Stop and evaluate at each point. Are your good deeds motivated by self-glory or God's glory? Pray about it. Are you growing in your knowledge of Him? Pray! Is God the source of your strength? Are you exhibiting patience as a result of your relationship with the Lord? Do you have joy as you give thanks? Give thanks!

9. Pray through the prayer again, this time on behalf of your family members, your local church, and the church around the world.

## THURSDAY: JESUS REVEALED

1. Prayerfully read the portion of Scripture that will be the focus of today's study.

> **Colossians 1:13** He delivered us from the power of darkness and transferred us to the kingdom of the Son he loves, 1:14 in whom we have redemption, the forgiveness of sins.

**1:15** He is the image of the invisible God, the firstborn over all creation,

**1:16** for all things in heaven and on earth were created by him—all things, whether visible or invisible, whether thrones or dominions, whether principalities or powers—all things were created through him and for him.

**1:17** He himself is before all things and all things are held together in him.

**1:18** He is the head of the body, the church, as well as the beginning, the firstborn from among the dead, so that he himself may become first in all things.

2. From what and to what have Christ-followers been delivered (1:13)? Note the past, not future, tense of the words.

_____

_____

_____

_____

3. Based on 1:13, how would you describe the relationship that exists between the Son and the Father?

_____

_____

_____

4. What two benefits that the Son has given to believers are mentioned in 1:14?

_____

_____

_____

• *In whom we have redemption.* Through the Son we have redemption. *Redeem* is a marketplace term meaning "to buy" or "buy out." To redeem a slave is to purchase that slave with the goal of setting him or her free. We will see the idea of redemption reappearing in Colossians 4:5, where Paul uses the word with *time*, "redeeming the time," which has the idea of buying up every opportunity and making the very most of it, since once it's spent, it's gone. Here Paul links redemption with forgiveness. All who believe in Christ have liberation *from* something (guilt, slavery) *to* something (newness of life and liberty).

5. If someone bought you out of a literal slave market, would you rebel against that person, or would you want to do all you could to express your gratitude? Why?

_____

_____

_____

6. Who is the Son, according to verse 15?

_____

_____

_____

• *Image.* If God created mankind in His image, what does it mean that Christ is the image, the *eikon*, of the invisible God? John 1:18 says that no one has ever seen God. How could we? He's invisible! Yet John also writes that Christ has made God known. The word *eikon* was used in Paul's day of a portrait. Yesterday I sent a photo file to a friend who has not seen me in four years. She will open it and think, *Sandi's aged*, because that image is an exact representation of my face when my husband snapped the shot recently, and I look older than I did four years ago. Yet that photo is not my face itself. It's not me, my person.

And that's where we run into a big difference. It's not enough to say that Jesus is the mirror image or even the photograph (to use a modern parallel) of God. He *is* the image! He is God!

In his commentary on Colossians and Philemon, Kent Hughes writes, "The image of God also carries the idea of revealing the personal character of God." [4] So Jesus is not a facsimile of God. He's not a photocopy or a photo. He is the revelation of who God is because, as He said, "The Father and I are one." We know from John 1 that "the Word was with God, and the Word was fully God. . . . The Word became flesh and took up residence among us. We saw his glory—the glory of the one and only, full of grace and truth, who came from the Father" (John 1:1, 14). Put that together with what we know from Philippians 2: Even though the Son was (and is) equal with God, He let go and took on flesh and humbled Himself for a time. Some say Jesus submitted to the Father because it's His function to be under the Father's authority. But that's not quite right. The language of the Father sending and the Son submitting comes after the events described in Philippians 2, after the humbling. *Obedient* does not describe what Jesus is for all eternity. Obey is what He did in time and space to purchase our redemption. How humble is the Son!

One night at bedtime I was praying with my daughter, and she asked a question: "How can Jesus be both God and God's Son?" Gulp. Uh, great question! My initial answer was that theologians have spent two thousand years wrestling with that mystery, and so far nobody has solved it! Later, though, we discussed how God is one but He is three persons—Father, Son, and Holy Spirit. The Father is not the Son or the Spirit, but the Father is God. The Son is not the Father or the Spirit, but the Son is God. The Spirit is not the Father or the Son, but the Spirit is God. In trying to draw comparisons, all our analogies fail. God is not like vapor, water, and ice. He's not like an egg white, an egg yolk, and a shell. He is only like . . . God.

Jesus is both divine and human. Some say He is only divine and not human. That's the Gnostic influence. They can't imagine how flesh could be sacred. At the other extreme are those who would strip Jesus of His divinity, saying He is only a good man but certainly not God in the flesh.

Jesus is both.

The Son in heaven, equal with God, emptied Himself and took on human flesh. And a day is coming when every knee will bow and every tongue confess that He is Lord.

- *Firstborn*. Jesus was Mary's firstborn son, but being firstborn

---

[4] Kent Hughes, *Colossians and Philemon* (Westchester: Crossway Books, 1989).

over all creation is something different entirely. While the word *first-born* can refer to something as first chronologically, it also has a use that's unrelated to birth order: preeminence. Clearly in this instance, it's the latter. We'll explore this more fully on Saturday, but note for now that in this passage Christ is said to be both firstborn of all creation and firstborn from the dead.

7. What has Christ created (1:16)?

_____

_____

_____

## The Nine Choirs of Angels

*Highest order; adore God; dwell in God's presence*
• *Seraphim*
• *Cherubim*
• Thrones

*Govern lesser choirs of angels; govern stars and planets; fight evil powers*
• Dominions
• *Virtues*
• Powers

*Oversight of nations and cities; deliver God's most important messages to humans; guard humans*
• Principalities
• *Archangels*
• *Angels (regular)*

*When we hear "Sing, choirs of angels" in the song "O Come, All Ye Faithful," we might picture a choir like a robed chorus in a church. Yet since the fourth century, theologians have identified nine types (or choirs) of angels, divided into three groups. Although not official dogma, this categorization became popular in the Middle Ages through the writings of Thomas Aquinas, Dante (see Paradiso, Canto xxviii), and others. Four of the choirs are mentioned in Colossians.*

• *Thrones or dominions, whether principalities or powers.* Compare this phrase in Colossians with Ephesians 6:12: "For our struggle is not against flesh and blood, but against the rulers, against the powers, against the world rulers of this darkness, against the spiritual forces of evil in the heavens." The words *thrones, dominions, principalities,* and *powers* in Colossians most likely relate to the spirit world.

8. How and why were all things created (1:16)?

_____

_____

_____

9. If Christ created all things—visible and invisible—what hope should that give us when we face unseen evil forces? (This is not to say that Jesus created them evil any more than He created us to be evil! They chose to rebel, but He is still their Maker.)

_____

_____

_____

Verse 18 says that Jesus is the head of the body, the church. Because we use the word *head* so much for "head of the company" or "head of the family," it's easy for us to picture this verse as an organizational chart (with a head and an assistant) or even to picture a leader in every instance where we hear the word, but in doing so we miss a beautiful metaphor.

Connect *head* with the other word Paul uses: *body.* Imagine a head connected to a body at the neck. What a picture of total oneness and interdependence! Each person is a member of Christ's body (a toe, a mouth, an ear), and collectively we make up the body, the church. Christ does not need the church to do His work in the world, yet He has chosen to use the church as His body—His own arms reaching out to hug the hurting nations; His feet through us taking the gospel to the world and "walking" worthy; His eyes weeping through us as we weep with those who weep; His hands offering through us a cup of water to a weary soul.

8. In addition to being head of the body, the church, what else does Paul say Christ is (1:18)? What do you think it means?

_____

_____

_____

*Firstborn* appears again, and note this time why Jesus is head and beginning and firstborn from the dead: that He might have preeminence in everything. Jesus is preeminent over the body. He is supreme over creation, He is supreme over time, and He is supreme even over death.

10. Jesus Christ created all things, and in Him all things hold together. Take a walk sometime this week for the express purpose of marveling at His creation and worshiping Him for what He has done. What day will you plan to take your walk? When you return, note your impressions.

_____

_____

_____

_____

11. List everything that is out of Christ's control and which we should fear.

_____

_____

1. Prayerfully and thoughtfully read and meditate on the passage for today.

> **Colossians 1:19** For God was pleased to have all his fullness dwell in the Son
>
> **1:20** and through him to reconcile all things to himself by making peace through the blood of his cross—through him, whether things on earth or things in heaven.
>
> **1:21** And you were at one time strangers and enemies in your minds as expressed through your evil deeds, **1:22** but now he has reconciled you by his physical body through death to present you holy, without blemish, and blameless before him—**1:23** if indeed you remain in the faith, established and firm, without shifting from the hope of the gospel that you heard. This gospel has also been preached in all creation under heaven, and I, Paul, have become its servant.

2. According to Colossians 1:19, where does all the fullness of God dwell? How does God feel about it?

_____

_____

_____

3. Name and describe a dramatic reconciliation you have seen or experienced. It can be from your own life, from that of a friend, or even from a film or TV show.

_____

_____

_____

_____

4. List some broken relationships that you long to see reconciled; then pray about them.

_____

_____

_____

_____

- *Reconcile.* Reconciliation is not just the absence of conflict but the establishment of a new relationship on a new basis. It's to change a relationship by establishing harmony in place of enmity, creating peace.
- *Making peace.* Colossians 1:20 says that through the Son's reconciling work, God made peace through the blood of the cross. Note that there's a major difference between making peace and keeping peace. Think of the UN peacekeeping forces—to keep the peace they have to tote guns! The kind of peace to which Paul refers is once for all.
- *Through the blood of the cross.* Jesus' blood alone is the currency of redemption. Not blood plus works, not works alone, but Jesus' blood alone. Are you trusting in Jesus' finished work to reconcile you to God? Are you aware enough of your own sin to recognize your need for reconciliation?

5. Remember back in Genesis when Adam sinned? God is the one who went looking for Adam. According to Colossians 1:19–20, who is the initiator of reconciliation with God?

_____

_____

6. Who is the peacemaker in this scenario (1:20)?

_____

_____

7. Who are the recipients of the peacemaking mission (1:20)?

_____

_____

8. According to 1:21, what two words describe the state of the Colossian Christians before they believed? Do you think this is true of all believers or Paul's immediate audience only? Why or why not?

_____

_____

_____

9. What was the evidence of the animosity (1:21)?

_____

_____

_____

10. In today's reading, circle the first two words in 1:22. Complete this chart contrasting then and now, using information from 1:21–22.

| Then | Now |
|------|-----|
| What they were: | What they are: |
| How expressed: | How reconciled: |
| | Why reconciled: |

11. How were and are we like the Colossian believers?

_____

12. Paul says that to be presented without blemish and blameless before the Lord, we must remain in the faith. What two phrases describe what that looks like (1:23)?

_____

_____

_____

## SATURDAY: FIRSTBORN BUT NOT BORN FIRST

Martha Washington. Abigail Adams. Eleanor Roosevelt. Bess Truman. Each of these women has been First Lady of the United States. Now, does *first lady* mean they arrived in the US before any other women? Of course not.

When Henry Lee described George Washington as "first in war, first in peace, and first in the hearts of his countrymen," did he mean George Washington was chronologically the first soldier, the first treaty writer, and the first person ever to endear himself to those he served? No way.

When a popular company's advertising slogan asserts "We're not first—you are," it certainly doesn't mean the company arrived at some unspecified destination after its customers did, does it? Not even close.

Similarly, when Paul tells the Colossian believers that Jesus is the firstborn over all creation, he does not mean that the baby Jesus was literally the first created thing to be born. Contrary to what some say, Jesus was not, in fact, created at all. As the Nicene Creed (AD 325) asserts and we sing in "O Come, All Ye Faithful," He is "very God, begotten, not created"! He entered a birth canal and He was born, but the Son of God was not created.

When Paul says "firstborn," he has in mind honor, preeminence, glory. First in importance.

The word for *firstborn* is *prototokos*. See the *proto* part? It's the prefix on words like *prototype*. *Prototokos* as it was used in Paul's day could refer to something first chronologically, such as "my firstborn child," the oldest kid in the family, but it also could refer to preeminence in rank.

Psalm 89:17–29 gives us an example of *firstborn* meaning "preeminent." The psalmist, apparently a writer named Ethan, is talking about God's faithfulness to Israel. Here's what he says:

**89:17** For you give them splendor and strength. By your favor we are victorious.

**89:18** For our shield belongs to the Lord, our king to the Holy One of Israel.

**89:19** Then you spoke through a vision to your faithful followers and said: "I have energized a warrior; I have raised up a young man from the people.

**89:20** I have discovered David, my servant. With my holy oil I have anointed him as king.

**89:21** My hand will support him, and my arm will strengthen him.

**89:22** No enemy will be able to exact tribute from him; a violent oppressor will not be able to humiliate him.

**89:23** I will crush his enemies before him; I will strike down those who hate him.

**89:24** He will experience my faithfulness and loyal love, and by my name he will win victories.

**89:25** I will place his hand over the sea, his right hand over the rivers.

**89:26** He will call out to me, 'You are my father, my God, and the protector who delivers me.'

**89:27** *I will appoint him to be my firstborn son, the most exalted of the earth's kings.*

**89:28** I will always extend my loyal love to him, and my covenant with him is secure.

**89:29** I will give him an eternal dynasty, and make his throne as enduring as the skies above.

Ethan quotes God talking about David. Notice what the Lord says: "I will appoint him to be my firstborn." I think it's safe to say that God does not mean for us to envision David crawling back into his mother's womb along with his brothers and entering the world first this time. And in Colossians 1:15, Paul is not emphasizing Jesus' birth order, as if God could have such a thing! Rather, Paul emphasizes that Jesus ranks above creation as Creator and sustainer of it all.

As firstborn in rank or honor, Jesus has no gods above Him. He didn't come from a long line of demigods, as Gnosticism claimed beginning late in the second century. (Gnostics believe that only a god removed from God could interact with matter—that is, take on human flesh—because they consider matter to be evil.)

Recently Jupiter, Mercury, and Mars appeared nestled so closely together in the sky that if you held up your thumb toward where they appeared, the width of your one finger could block out your view of all three. It was the first time in eighty years these three planets had been that close in the sky, though they were still millions upon millions of miles away from each other. I love how Miami's Space Transit Planetarium director described this rare triple-planetary treat: "It is a lovely demonstration of the celestial ballet that goes on around us, day after day, year after year, millennium after millennium. When I look at something like this, I realize that all the powers on Earth, all the emperors, all the money, cannot change it one iota. We are observers, but the wonderful part of that is that we are the only species on this planet that can observe it and understand it."

That celestial ballet? Christ made it all. And His creation included us in God's image—which is why we're the only species on the planet that can understand that "the heavens declare the glory of God" (Ps. 19:1). He rules over it all. What a wonderful Savior!

**Prayer:** *Father, thank You for Your initiative in pursuing me, as revealed in Your Son, bringing reconciliation. I admit my desperate need for You. Please help me to see myself and my circumstances through Your eyes. Let me see You in the pages of Your Word, and help me to reflect what I see by the way I live. Even in my limited understanding of You, I adore You for who You are. Thank You for sending Your Son, through whom all things hold together. In His name I pray, Amen.*

**For Memorization:** "He is the image of the invisible God, the firstborn over all creation, for all things in heaven and on earth were created by him—all things, whether visible or invisible, whether thrones or dominions, whether principalities or powers—all things were created through him and for him. He himself is before all things and all things are held together in him. He is the head of the body, the church, as well as the beginning, the firstborn from among the dead, so that he himself may become first in all things." (Col. 1:15–18)

# WEEK 2 OF 4

## *Christ the Fullness of Deity: Colossians 1:24–2:23*

## SUNDAY: CHECK IT OUT

**Scripture:** "He himself is before all things and all things are held together in him." (Col. 1:17)

Every year my twenty-something dorm-mom friend, Greta, makes it her goal to read at least fifty books. (She finished her fiftieth with about an hour to spare last year.) Greta reads from the best-seller list and she reads classics; she reads nonfiction and she reads fiction. As a result she can quote Aristotle in the same sentence that she mentions Stephen King. She's a fascinating conversationalist.

Not long ago, Greta and her husband, Benji, decided to read texts from classic sermons. Later, when they compared notes, they realized that both of them were awed by a message Jonathan Edwards preached in 1746. In fact, Greta said, they were "gleefully stumbling over and discussing the same passage." The sermon was titled "The

Excellency of Christ." Here is the NET rendering of the text, Colossians 1:15–20, on which Edwards based his message:

> **Colossians 1:15** He is the image of the invisible God, the first-born over all creation, **1:16** for all things in heaven and on earth were created by him—all things, whether visible or invisible, whether thrones or dominions, whether principalities or powers—all things were created through him and for him. **1:17** He himself is before all things and all things are held together in him. **1:18** He is the head of the body, the church, as well as the beginning, the first-born from among the dead, so that he himself may become first in all things. **1:19** For God was pleased to have all his fullness dwell in the Son **1:20** and through him to reconcile all things to himself by making peace through the blood of his cross—through him, whether things on earth or things in heaven.

Here's what Edwards wrote that left Greta and her husband in such awe: "What is there that you can desire should be in a Savior that is not in Christ? Or, wherein should you desire a Savior should be otherwise than Christ is? What excellency is there wanting? What is there that is great or good? What is there that is venerable or winning? What is there that is adorable or endearing? Or, what can you think of, that would be encouraging, that is not to be found in the person of Christ? . . . What is there wanting, or what would you add if you could, to make him more fit to be your Savior?"

"I've been thinking about it ever since," Greta said. "Everything I need my Savior to be, Christ is or has been. Holy? Check. Human? Check. Loving? Check. Near to God? Check. Check. Check. Check. Check. Check. What a joyful comfort to my soul that my Savior is so incredibly and completely everything I need."

As if that weren't enough, we even could add to Greta's list, couldn't we? Creator and sustainer of the universe? Check. Approachable? Check. Transcendent? Check. Forgiving? Double check. Able to overpower evil forces? A reconciler? Check squared. Check cubed. Exponential check. Check to the tenth checked power. Our Savior and His story are as good as it gets.

It should not surprise us, then, that the realization of this truth led to the conversion of C. S. Lewis of Narnia fame. An Oxford don with an impressive grasp of Norse mythology, Lewis was familiar with pagan myths full of heroism, selflessness, dying saviors, and resurrections. Yet Lewis told his friend, J. R. R. Tolkien, author of *The Hobbit* and *The*

*Lord of the Rings*, that myths were "lies and therefore worthless, even though breathed through silver."

Tolkien disagreed. He insisted that myths are not lies, but rather the best if not the only way to convey truths that would otherwise remain inexpressible. Humans created in God's image, Tolkien reasoned, weave myths as a reflection of our original glory. Through poets' stories, fragments of eternal light shine through. For that reason, Tolkien said, myths, though misguided, can steer us in the journey toward the ultimate story told in Jesus Christ. Through the story of Jesus, God manifested Himself "through Himself, with Himself, and in Himself. God, in the Incarnation, had revealed Himself as the ultimate poet who was creating reality, the true poem or true myth, in His own image. Thus, in a divinely inspired paradox, myth was revealed as the ultimate realism."[5]

The best fiction human minds can construe becomes reality in the person of Jesus Christ. The king leaves the throne room, He becomes like His pauper subjects, and He dies on their behalf. Then He comes back to life, adopts the paupers as His children, and, riding on a white horse, He conquers all His enemies until all the kingdoms of the world acknowledge Him as "King of Kings and Lord of Lords" (Rev. 19:16).

Do you know Christ? What more do you need in a Savior? Does your life show how much you appreciate Him?

## MONDAY: THE LETTER

1. Ask for God's Spirit to give you wisdom, insight, and illumination. Then read Colossians 1:24–2:23, which will be our focus for this week.

> **Colossians 1:24** Now I rejoice in my sufferings for you, and I fill up in my physical body—for the sake of his body, the church—what is lacking in the sufferings of Christ. **1:25** I became a servant of the church according to the stewardship from God—given to me for you—in order to complete the word of God, **1:26** that is, the mystery that has been kept hidden from ages and generations, but has now been revealed to his saints. **1:27** God wanted to make known to them the glorious riches of this mystery among the Gentiles, which

---

[5] Joseph Pearce, "J. R. R. Tolkien: Truth and Myth," http://www.catholiceducation.org, accessed December 13, 2006.

is Christ in you, the hope of glory. **1:28** We proclaim him by instructing and teaching all people with all wisdom so that we may present every person mature in Christ. **1:29** Toward this goal I also labor, struggling according to his power that powerfully works in me.

**2:1** For I want you to know how great a struggle I have for you, and for those in Laodicea, and for those who have not met me face to face. **2:2** My goal is that their hearts, having been knit together in love, may be encouraged, and that they may have all the riches that assurance brings in their understanding of the knowledge of the mystery of God, namely, Christ, **2:3** in whom are hidden all the treasures of wisdom and knowledge. **2:4** I say this so that no one will deceive you through arguments that sound reasonable. **2:5** For though I am absent from you in body, I am present with you in spirit, rejoicing to see your morale and the firmness of your faith in Christ.

**2:6** Therefore, just as you received Christ Jesus as Lord, continue to live your lives in him, **2:7** rooted and built up in him and firm in your faith just as you were taught, and overflowing with thankfulness. **2:8** Be careful not to allow anyone to captivate you through an empty, deceitful philosophy that is according to human traditions and the elemental spirits of the world, and not according to Christ. **2:9** For in him all the fullness of deity lives in bodily form, **2:10** and you have been filled in him, who is the head over every ruler and authority. **2:11** In him you also were circumcised—not, however, with a circumcision performed by human hands, but by the removal of the fleshly body, that is, through the circumcision done by Christ. **2:12** Having been buried with him in baptism, you also have been raised with him through your faith in the power of God who raised him from the dead. **2:13** And even though you were dead in your transgressions and in the uncircumcision of your flesh, he nevertheless made you alive with him, having forgiven all your transgressions. **2:14** He has destroyed what was against us, a certificate of indebtedness expressed in decrees opposed to us. He has taken it away by nailing it to the cross. **2:15** Disarming the rulers and authorities, he has made a public disgrace of them, triumphing over them by the cross.

**2:16** Therefore do not let anyone judge you with respect to food or drink, or in the matter of a feast, new moon, or Sabbath days—**2:17** these are only the shadow of the things to come, but the reality is Christ! **2:18** Let no one who delights in humility and the worship of angels pass judgment on you. That person goes on at great lengths about what he has supposedly seen, but he is puffed up with empty notions by his fleshly mind. **2:19** He has not held fast to the head from whom the whole body, supported and knit together through its ligaments and sinews, grows with a growth that is from God.

**2:20** If you have died with Christ to the elemental spirits of the world, why do you submit to them as though you lived in the world? **2:21** "Do not handle! Do not taste! Do not touch!" **2:22** These are all destined to perish with use, founded as they are on human commands and teachings. **2:23** Even though they have the appearance of wisdom with their self-imposed worship and false humility achieved by an unsparing treatment of the body—a wisdom with no true value—they in reality result in fleshly indulgence.

2. Note any observations you made as you read.

_____

_____

_____

3. What stands out to you as being of primary concern to Paul?

_____

_____

4. What questions did you ask as you read? (Do you wonder what could be "lacking in the sufferings of Christ"?)

_____

_____

_____

5. Summarize what you think Paul is trying to say.

_____

_____

_____

To get the background on why Paul is imprisoned, read Luke's account of events as recorded in Acts 21:17–28:30. As you read, circle every reference to the Gentiles.

**Acts 21:17** When we arrived in Jerusalem, the brothers welcomed us gladly. **21:18** The next day Paul went in with us to see James, and all the elders were there. **21:19** When Paul had greeted them, he began to explain in detail what God had done among the Gentiles through his ministry. **21:20** When they heard this, they praised God. Then they said to him, "You see, brother, how many thousands of Jews there are who have believed, and they are all ardent observers of the law. **21:21** They have been informed about you—that you teach all the Jews now living among the Gentiles to abandon Moses, telling them not to circumcise their children or live according to our customs. **21:22** What then should we do? They will no doubt hear that you have come. **21:23** So do what we tell you: We have four men who have taken a vow; **21:24** take them and purify yourself along with them and pay their expenses, so that they may have their heads shaved. Then everyone will know there is nothing in what they have been told about you, but that you yourself live in conformity with the law. **21:25** But regarding the Gentiles who have believed, we have written a letter, having decided that they should avoid meat that has been sacrificed to idols and blood and what has been strangled and sexual immorality." **21:26** Then Paul took the men the next day, and after he had purified himself along with them, he went to the temple and gave notice of the completion of the days of purification, when the sacrifice would be offered for each of them. **21:27** When the seven days were almost over, the Jews from the province of Asia who had seen him in the temple area stirred up the whole crowd and seized him, **21:28** shouting, "Men of Israel, help! This is the man who teaches everyone everywhere against our people, our law, and this sanctuary! Furthermore he has brought Greeks into the inner courts of the temple and made this holy place ritually unclean!" **21:29** (For they had seen Trophimus the Ephesian in the city with him previously, and they assumed Paul had brought him into the inner temple courts.) **21:30** The whole city was stirred up, and the people rushed together. They seized Paul and dragged him out of the temple courts, and immediately the doors were shut. **21:31** While they were trying to kill him, a report was sent up to the commanding officer of the cohort that all Jerusalem was in confusion. **21:32** He immediately took soldiers and centurions and ran down to the crowd. When they saw the commanding officer and the soldiers, they stopped beating Paul. **21:33** Then the commanding officer came up and arrested him and ordered him to be tied up with two chains; he then asked who he was and what he had done. **21:34** But some in the crowd shouted one thing, and others something else, and when the commanding officer was unable to find out the truth because of the disturbance, he ordered Paul to be brought into the barracks. **21:35** When he came to the steps, Paul had to be carried by the soldiers because of the violence of the mob, **21:36** for a crowd of people followed them, screaming, "Away with him!" **21:37** As Paul was about to be brought into the barracks, he said to the commanding officer, "May I say something to you?" The officer replied, "Do you know Greek? **21:38** Then you're not that Egyptian who started a rebellion and led the four thousand men of the 'Assassins' into the wilderness some time ago?" **21:39** Paul answered, "I am a Jew from Tarsus in Cilicia, a citizen of an important city. Please allow me to speak to the people." **21:40** When the commanding officer had given him permission, Paul stood on the steps and gestured to the people with his hand. When they had become silent, he addressed them in Aramaic,

## Acts 22

**22:1** "Brothers and fathers, listen to my defense that I now make to you." **22:2** (When they heard that he was addressing them in Aramaic, they became even quieter.) Then Paul said, **22:3** "I am a Jew, born in Tarsus in Cilicia, but brought up in this city, educated with strictness under Gamaliel according to the law of our ancestors, and was zealous for God just as all of you are today. **22:4** I persecuted this Way even to the point of death, tying up both men and women and putting them in prison, **22:5** as both the high priest and the whole council of elders can testify about me. From them I also received letters to the brothers in Damascus, and I was on my way to make arrests there and bring the prisoners to Jerusalem to be punished. **22:6** As I was en route and near Damascus, about noon a very bright light from heaven suddenly flashed around me. **22:7** Then I fell to the ground and heard a voice saying to me, 'Saul, Saul, why are you persecuting me?' **22:8** I answered, 'Who are you, Lord?' He said to me, 'I am Jesus the Nazarene, whom you are persecuting.' **22:9** Those who were with me saw the light, but did not understand the voice of the one who was speaking to me. **22:10** So I asked, 'What should I do, Lord?' The Lord said to me, 'Get up and go to Damascus; there you will be told about everything that you have been designated to do! **22:11** Since I could not see because of the brilliance of that light, I came to Damascus led by the hand of those who were with me. **22:12** A man named Ananias, a devout man according to the law, well spoken of by all the Jews who live there, **22:13** came to me and stood beside me and said to me, 'Brother Saul, regain your sight!' And at that very moment I looked up and saw him. **22:14** Then he said, 'The God of our ancestors has already chosen you to know his will, to see the Righteous One, and to hear a command from his mouth, **22:15** because you will be his witness to all people of what you have seen and heard. **22:16** And now what are you waiting for? Get up, be baptized, and have your sins washed away, calling on his name! **22:17** When I returned to Jerusalem and was praying in the temple, I fell into a trance **22:18** and saw the Lord saying to me, 'Hurry and get out of Jerusalem quickly, because they will not accept your testimony about me! **22:19** I replied, 'Lord, they themselves know that I imprisoned and beat those in the various synagogues who believed in you. **22:20** And when the blood of your witness Stephen was shed, I myself was standing nearby, approving, and guarding the cloaks of those who were killing him! **22:21** Then he said to me, 'Go, because I will send you far away to the Gentiles.'"

**22:22** The crowd was listening to him until he said this. Then they raised their voices and shouted, "Away with this man from the earth! For he should not be allowed to live!" **22:23** While they were screaming and throwing off their cloaks and tossing dust in the air, **22:24** the commanding officer ordered Paul to be brought back into the barracks. He told them to interrogate Paul by beating him with a lash so that he could find out the reason the crowd was shouting at Paul in this way. **22:25** When they had stretched him out for the lash, Paul said to the centurion standing nearby, "Is it legal for you to lash a man who is a Roman citizen without a proper trial?" **22:26** When the centurion heard this, he went to the commanding officer and reported it, saying, "What are you about to do? For this man is a Roman citizen." **22:27** So the commanding officer came and asked Paul, "Tell me, are you a Roman citizen?" He replied, "Yes." **22:28** The commanding officer answered, "I acquired this citizenship with a large sum of money." "But I was even born a citizen," Paul replied. **22:29** Then those who were about to interrogate him stayed away from him, and the commanding officer was frightened when he realized that Paul was a Roman citizen and that he had had him tied up.

**22:30** The next day, because the commanding officer wanted to know the true reason Paul was being accused by the Jews, he released him and ordered the chief priests and the whole council to assemble. He then brought Paul down and had him stand before them.

## Acts 23

**23:1** Paul looked directly at the council and said, "Brothers, I have lived my life with a clear conscience before God to this day." **23:2** At that the high priest Ananias ordered those standing near Paul to strike him on the mouth. **23:3** Then Paul said to him, "God is going to strike you, you whitewashed wall! Do you sit there judging me according to the law, and in violation of the law you order me to be struck?" **23:4** Those standing near him said, "Do you dare insult God's high priest?" **23:5** Paul replied, "I did not realize, brothers, that he was the high priest, for it is written, 'You must not speak evil about a ruler of your people.' "

**23:6** Then when Paul noticed that part of them were Sadducees and the others Pharisees, he shouted out in the council, "Brothers, I am a Pharisee, a son of Pharisees. I am on trial concerning the hope of the resurrection of the dead!" **23:7** When he said this, an argument began between the Pharisees and the Sadducees, and the assembly was divided. **23:8** (For the Sadducees say there is no resurrection, or angel, or spirit, but the Pharisees acknowledge them all.) **23:9** There was a great commotion, and some experts in the law from the party of the Pharisees stood up and protested strongly, "We find nothing wrong with this man. What if a spirit or an angel has spoken to him?" **23:10** When the argument became so great the commanding officer feared that they would tear Paul to pieces, he ordered the detachment to go down, take him away from them by force, and bring him into the barracks.

**23:11** The following night the Lord stood near Paul and said, "Have courage, for just as you have testified about me in Jerusalem, so you must also testify in Rome."

**23:12** When morning came, the Jews formed a conspiracy and bound themselves with an oath not to eat or drink anything until they had killed Paul. **23:13** There were more than forty of them who formed this conspiracy. **23:14** They went to the chief priests and the elders and said, "We have bound ourselves with a solemn oath not to partake of anything until we have killed Paul. **23:15** So now you and the council request the commanding officer to bring him down to you, as if you were going to determine his case by conducting a more thorough inquiry. We are ready to kill him before he comes near this place."

**23:16** But when the son of Paul's sister heard about the ambush, he came and entered the barracks and told Paul. **23:17** Paul called one of the centurions and said, "Take this young man to the commanding officer, for he has something to report to him."

**23:18** So the centurion took him and brought him to the commanding officer and said, "The prisoner Paul called me and asked me to bring this young man to you because he has something to tell you." **23:19** The commanding officer took him by the hand, withdrew privately, and asked, "What is it that you want to report to me?" **23:20** He replied, "The Jews have agreed to ask you to bring Paul down to the council tomorrow, as if they were going to inquire more thoroughly about him. **23:21** So do not let them persuade you to do this, because more than forty of them are lying in ambush for him. They have bound themselves with an oath not to eat or drink anything until they have killed him, and now they are ready, waiting for you to agree to their request." **23:22** Then the commanding officer sent the young man away, directing him, "Tell no one that you have reported these things to me." **23:23** Then he summoned two of the centurions and said, "Make ready two hundred soldiers to go to Caesarea along with seventy horsemen and two hundred spearmen by nine o'clock tonight, **23:24** and provide mounts for Paul to ride so that he may be brought safely to Felix the governor." **23:25** He wrote a letter that went like this:

**23:26** Claudius Lysias to His Excellency Governor Felix, greetings. **23:27** This man was seized by the Jews and they were about to kill him, when I came up with the detachment and rescued him, because I had learned that he was a Roman citizen. **23:28** Since I wanted to know what charge they were accusing him of, I brought him down to their council. **23:29** I found he was accused with reference to controversial questions about their law, but no charge against him deserved death or imprisonment. **23:30** When I was informed there would be a plot against this man, I sent him to you at once, also ordering his accusers to state their charges against him before you.

**23:31** So the soldiers, in accordance with their orders, took Paul and brought him to Antipatris during the night. **23:32** The next day they let the horsemen go on with him, and they returned to the barracks. **23:33** When the horsemen came to Caesarea and delivered the letter to the governor, they also presented Paul to him. **23:34** When the governor had read the letter, he asked what province he was from. When he learned that he was from Cilicia, **23:35** he said, "I will give you a hearing when your accusers arrive too." Then he ordered that Paul be kept under guard in Herod's palace.

## Acts 24

**24:1** After five days the high priest Ananias came down with some elders and an attorney named Tertullus, and they brought formal charges against Paul to the governor. **24:2** When Paul had been summoned, Tertullus began to accuse him, saying, "We have experienced a lengthy time of peace through your rule, and reforms are being made in this nation through your foresight. **24:3** Most excellent Felix, we acknowledge this everywhere and in every way with all gratitude. **24:4** But so that I may not delay you any further, I beg you to hear us briefly with your customary graciousness. **24:5** For we have found this man to be a troublemaker, one who stirs up riots among all the Jews throughout the world, and a ringleader of the sect of the Nazarenes. **24:6** He even tried to desecrate the temple, so we arrested him. **24:8** When you examine him yourself, you will be able to learn from him about all these things we are accusing him of doing." **24:9** The Jews also joined in the verbal attack, claiming that these things were true.

**24:10** When the governor gestured for him to speak, Paul replied, "Because I know that you have been a judge over this nation for many years, I confidently make my defense. **24:11** As you can verify for yourself, not more than twelve days ago I went up to Jerusalem to worship. **24:12** They did not find me arguing with anyone or stirring up a crowd in the temple courts or in the synagogues or throughout the city, **24:13** nor can they prove to you the things they are accusing me of doing. **24:14** But I confess this to you, that I worship the God of our ancestors according to the Way (which they call a sect), believing everything that is according to the law and that is written in the prophets. **24:15** I have a hope in God (a hope that these men themselves accept too) that there is going to be a resurrection of both the righteous and the unrighteous. **24:16** This is the reason I do my best to always have a clear conscience toward God and toward people. **24:17** After several years I came to bring to my people gifts for the poor and to present offerings, **24:18** which I was doing when they found me in the temple, ritually purified, without a crowd or a disturbance. **24:19** But there are some Jews from the province of Asia who should be here before you and bring charges, if they have anything against me. **24:20** Or these men here should tell what crime they found me guilty of when I stood before the council, **24:21** other than this one thing I shouted out while I stood before them: 'I am on trial before you today concerning the resurrection of the dead.'"

**24:22** Then Felix, who understood the facts concerning the Way more accurately, adjourned their hearing, saying, "When Lysias the commanding officer comes down, I will decide your case." **24:23** He ordered the centurion to guard Paul, but to let him have some freedom, and not to prevent any of his friends from meeting his needs.

**24:24** Some days later, when Felix arrived with his wife Drusilla, who was Jewish, he sent for Paul and heard him speak about faith in Christ Jesus. **24:25** While Paul was discussing righteousness, self-control, and the coming judgment, Felix became frightened and said, "Go away for now, and when I have an opportunity, I will send for you." **24:26** At the same time he was also hoping that Paul would give him money, and for this reason he sent for Paul as often as possible and talked with him. **24:27** After two years had passed, Porcius Festus succeeded Felix, and because he wanted to do the Jews a favor, Felix left Paul in prison.

## Acts 25

**25:1** Now three days after Festus arrived in the province, he went up to Jerusalem from Caesarea. **25:2** So the chief priests and the most prominent men of the Jews brought formal charges against Paul to him. **25:3** Requesting him to do them a favor against Paul, they urged Festus to summon him to Jerusalem, planning an ambush to kill him along the way. **25:4** Then Festus replied that Paul was being kept at Caesarea, and he himself intended to go there shortly. **25:5** "So," he said, "let your leaders go down there with me, and if this man has done anything wrong, they may bring charges against him."

**25:6** After Festus had stayed not more than eight or ten days among them, he went down to Caesarea, and the next day he sat on the judgment seat and ordered Paul to be brought. **25:7** When he arrived, the Jews who had come down from Jerusalem stood around him, bringing many serious charges that they were not able to prove. **25:8** Paul said in his defense, "I have committed no offense against the Jewish law or against the temple or against Caesar." **25:9** But Festus, wanting to do the Jews a favor, asked Paul, "Are you willing to go up to Jerusalem and be tried before me there on these charges?" **25:10** Paul replied, "I am standing before Caesar's judgment seat, where I should be tried. I have done nothing wrong to the Jews, as you also know very well. **25:11** If then I am in the wrong and have done anything that deserves death, I am not trying to escape dying, but if not one of their charges against me is true, no one can hand me over to them. I appeal to Caesar!" **25:12** Then, after conferring with his council, Festus replied, "You have appealed to Caesar; to Caesar you will go!"

**25:13** After several days had passed, King Agrippa and Bernice arrived at Caesarea to pay their respects to Festus. **25:14** While they were staying there many days, Festus explained Paul's case to the king to get his opinion, saying, "There is a man left here as a prisoner by Felix. **25:15** When I was in Jerusalem, the chief priests and the elders of the Jews informed me about him, asking for a sentence of condemnation against him. **25:16** I answered them that it was not the custom of the Romans to hand over anyone before the accused had met his accusers face to face and had been given an opportunity to make a defense against the accusation. **25:17** So after they came back here with me, I did not postpone the case, but the next day I sat on the judgment seat and ordered the man to be brought. **25:18** When his accusers stood up, they did not charge him with any of the evil deeds I had suspected. **25:19** Rather they had several points of disagreement with him about their own religion and about a man named Jesus who was dead, whom Paul claimed to be alive. **25:20** Because I was at a loss how I could investigate these matters, I asked if he were willing to go to Jerusalem and be tried there on these charges. **25:21** But when Paul appealed to be kept in custody for the decision of His Majesty the Emperor, I ordered him to be kept under guard until I could send him to Caesar." **25:22** Agrippa said to Festus, "I would also like to hear the man myself." "Tomorrow," he replied, "you will hear him."

**25:23** So the next day Agrippa and Bernice came with great pomp and entered the audience hall, along with the senior military officers and the prominent men of the city. When Festus gave the order, Paul was brought in. **25:24** Then Festus said, "King Agrippa, and all you who are present here with us, you see this man about whom the entire Jewish populace petitioned me both in Jerusalem and here, shouting loudly that he ought not to live any longer. **25:25** But I found that he had done nothing that deserved death, and when he appealed to His Majesty the Emperor, I decided to send him. **25:26** But I have nothing definite to write to my lord about him. Therefore I have brought him before you all, and especially before you, King Agrippa, so that after this preliminary hearing I may have something to write. **25:27** For it seems unreasonable to me to send a prisoner without clearly indicating the charges against him."

## Acts 26

**26:1** So Agrippa said to Paul, "You have permission to speak for yourself." Then Paul held out his hand and began his defense:

**26:2** "Regarding all the things I have been accused of by the Jews, King Agrippa, I consider myself fortunate that I am about to make my defense before you today, **26:3** because you are especially familiar with all the customs and controversial issues of the Jews.

Therefore I ask you to listen to me patiently. **26:4** Now all the Jews know the way I lived from my youth, spending my life from the beginning among my own people and in Jerusalem. **26:5** They know, because they have known me from time past, if they are willing to testify, that according to the strictest party of our religion, I lived as a Pharisee. **26:6** And now I stand here on trial because of my hope in the promise made by God to our ancestors, **26:7** a promise that our twelve tribes hope to attain as they earnestly serve God night and day. Concerning this hope the Jews are accusing me, Your Majesty! **26:8** Why do you people think it is unbelievable that God raises the dead? **26:9** Of course, I myself was convinced that it was necessary to do many things hostile to the name of Jesus the Nazarene. **26:10** And that is what I did in Jerusalem: Not only did I lock up many of the saints in prisons by the authority I received from the chief priests, but I also cast my vote against them when they were sentenced to death. **26:11** I punished them often in all the synagogues and tried to force them to blaspheme. Because I was so furiously enraged at them, I went to persecute them even in foreign cities.

**26:12** "While doing this very thing, as I was going to Damascus with authority and complete power from the chief priests, **26:13** about noon along the road, Your Majesty, I saw a light from heaven, brighter than the sun, shining everywhere around me and those traveling with me. **26:14** When we had all fallen to the ground, I heard a voice saying to me in Aramaic, 'Saul, Saul, why are you persecuting me? You are hurting yourself by kicking against the goads.' **26:15** So I said, 'Who are you, Lord?' And the Lord replied, 'I am Jesus whom you are persecuting. **26:16** But get up and stand on your feet, for I have appeared to you for this reason, to designate you in advance as a servant and witness to the things you have seen and to the things in which I will appear to you. **26:17** I will rescue you from your own people and from the Gentiles, to whom I am sending you **26:18** to open their eyes so that they turn from darkness to light and from the power of Satan to God, so that they may receive forgiveness of sins and a share among those who are sanctified by faith in me.'

**26:19** "Therefore, King Agrippa, I was not disobedient to the heavenly vision, **26:20** but I declared to those in Damascus first, and then to those in Jerusalem and in all Judea, and to the Gentiles, that they should repent and turn to God, performing deeds consistent with repentance. **26:21** For this reason the Jews seized me in the temple courts and were trying to kill me. **26:22** I have experienced help from God to this day, and so I stand testifying to both small and great, saying nothing except what the prophets and Moses said was going to happen: **26:23** that the Christ was to suffer and be the first to rise from the dead, to proclaim light both to our people and to the Gentiles."

**26:24** As Paul was saying these things in his defense, Festus exclaimed loudly, "You have lost your mind, Paul! Your great learning is driving you insane!" **26:25** But Paul replied, "I have not lost my mind, most excellent Festus, but am speaking true and rational words. **26:26** For the king knows about these things, and I am speaking freely to him, because I cannot believe that any of these things has escaped his notice, for this was not done in a corner. **26:27** Do you believe the prophets, King Agrippa? I know that you believe." **26:28** Agrippa said to Paul, "In such a short time are you persuading me to become a Christian?" **26:29** Paul replied, "I pray to God that whether in a short or a long time not only you but also all those who are listening to me today could become such as I am, except for these chains."

**26:30** So the king got up, and with him the governor and Bernice and those sitting with them, **26:31** and as they were leaving they said to one another, "This man is not doing anything deserving death or imprisonment." **26:32** Agrippa said to Festus, "This man could have been released if he had not appealed to Caesar."

## Acts 27

**27:1** When it was decided we would sail to Italy, they handed over Paul and some other prisoners to a centurion of the Augustan Cohort named Julius. **27:2** We went on board a ship from Adramyttium that was about to sail to various ports along the coast of the province of Asia and put out to sea, accompanied by Aristarchus, a Macedonian from Thessalonica. **27:3** The next day we put in at Sidon, and Julius, treating Paul kindly, allowed him to go to his friends so they could provide him with what he needed. **27:4** From there we put out to sea and sailed under the lee of Cyprus because the winds were against us. **27:5** After we had sailed across the open sea off Cilicia and Pamphylia, we put in at Myra in Lycia. **27:6** There the centurion found a ship from Alexandria sailing for Italy, and he put us aboard it. **27:7** We sailed slowly for many days and arrived with difficulty off Cnidus. Because the wind prevented us from going any farther, we sailed under the lee of Crete off Salmone. **27:8** With difficulty we sailed along the coast of Crete and came to a place called Fair Havens that was near the town of Lasea.

**27:9** Since considerable time had passed and the voyage was now dangerous because the fast was already over, Paul advised them, **27:10** "Men, I can see the voyage is going to end in disaster and great loss not only of the cargo and the ship, but also of our lives." **27:11** But the centurion was more convinced by the captain and the ship's owner than by what Paul said. **27:12** Because the harbor was not suitable to spend the winter in, the majority decided to put out to sea from there. They hoped that somehow they could reach Phoenix, a harbor of Crete facing southwest and northwest, and spend the winter there. **27:13** When a gentle south wind sprang up, they thought they could carry out their purpose, so they weighed anchor and sailed close along the coast of Crete. **27:14** Not long after this, a hurricane-force wind called the northeaster blew down from the island. **27:15** When the ship was caught in it and could not head into the wind, we gave way to it and were driven along. **27:16** As we ran under the lee of a small island called Cauda, we were able with difficulty to get the ship's boat under control. **27:17** After the crew had hoisted it aboard, they used supports to undergird the ship. Fearing they would run aground on the Syrtis, they lowered the sea anchor, thus letting themselves be driven along. **27:18** The next day, because we were violently battered by the storm, they began throwing the cargo overboard, **27:19** and on the third day they threw the ship's gear overboard with their own hands. **27:20** When neither sun nor stars appeared for many days and a violent storm continued to batter us, we finally abandoned all hope of being saved.

**27:21** Since many of them had no desire to eat, Paul stood up among them and said, "Men, you should have listened to me and not put out to sea from Crete, thus avoiding this damage and loss. **27:22** And now I advise you to keep up your courage, for there will be no loss of life among you, but only the ship will be lost. **27:23** For last night an angel of the God to whom I belong and whom I serve came to me **27:24** and said, 'Do not be afraid, Paul! You must stand before Caesar, and God has graciously granted you the safety of all who are sailing with you.' **27:25** Therefore keep up your courage, men, for I have faith in God that it will be just as I have been told. **27:26** But we must run aground on some island."

**27:27** When the fourteenth night had come, while we were being driven across the Adriatic Sea, about midnight the sailors suspected they were approaching some land. **27:28** They took soundings and found the water was twenty fathoms deep; when they had sailed a little farther they took soundings again and found it was fifteen fathoms deep. **27:29** Because they were afraid that we would run aground on the rocky coast, they threw out four anchors from the stern and wished for day to appear. **27:30** Then when the sailors tried to escape from the ship and were lowering the ship's boat into the sea, pretending that they were going to put out anchors from the bow, **27:31** Paul said to the centurion and the soldiers, "Unless these men stay with the ship, you cannot be saved." **27:32** Then the soldiers cut the ropes of the ship's boat and let it drift away.

**27:33** As day was about to dawn, Paul urged them all to take some food, saying, "Today is the fourteenth day you have been in suspense and have gone without food; you have eaten nothing. **27:34** Therefore I urge you to take some food, for this is important for your survival. For not one of you will lose a hair from his head." **27:35** After he said this, Paul took bread and gave thanks to God in front of them all, broke it, and began to eat. **27:36** So all of them were encouraged and took food themselves. **27:37** (We were in all two hundred seventy-six persons on the ship.) **27:38** When they had eaten enough to be satisfied, they lightened the ship by throwing the wheat into the sea.

**27:39** When day came, they did not recognize the land, but they noticed a bay with a beach, where they decided to run the ship aground if they could. **27:40** So they slipped the anchors and left them in the sea, at the same time loosening the linkage that bound the steering oars together. Then they hoisted the foresail to the wind and steered toward the beach. **27:41** But they encountered a patch of crosscurrents and ran the ship aground; the bow stuck fast and could not be moved, but the stern was being broken up by the force of the waves. **27:42** Now the soldiers' plan was to kill the prisoners so that none of them would escape by swimming away. **27:43** But the centurion, wanting to save Paul's life, prevented them from carrying out their plan. He ordered those who could swim to jump overboard first and get to land, **27:44** and the rest were to follow, some on planks and some on pieces of the ship. And in this way all were brought safely to land.

## Acts 28

**28:1** After we had safely reached shore, we learned that the island was called Malta. **28:2** The local inhabitants showed us extraordinary kindness, for they built a fire and welcomed us all because it had started to rain and was cold. **28:3** When Paul had gathered a bundle of brushwood and was putting it on the fire, a viper came out because of the heat and fastened itself on his hand. **28:4** When the local people saw the creature hanging from Paul's hand, they said to one another, "No doubt this man is a murderer! Although he has escaped from the sea, Justice herself has not allowed him to live!" **28:5** However, Paul shook the creature off into the fire and suffered no harm. **28:6** But they were expecting that he was going to swell up or suddenly drop dead. So after they had waited a long time and had seen nothing unusual happen to him, they changed their minds and said he was a god.

**28:7** Now in the region around that place were fields belonging to the chief official of the island, named Publius, who welcomed us and entertained us hospitably as guests for three days. **28:8** The father of Publius lay sick in bed, suffering from fever and dysentery. Paul went in to see him and after praying, placed his hands on him and healed him. **28:9** After this had happened, many of the people on the island who were sick also came and were healed. **28:10** They also bestowed many honors, and when we were preparing to sail, they gave us all the supplies we needed.

**28:11** After three months we put out to sea in an Alexandrian ship that had wintered at the island and had the "Heavenly Twins" as its figurehead. **28:12** We put in at Syracuse and stayed there three days. **28:13** From there we cast off and arrived at Rhegium, and after one day a south wind sprang up and on the second day we came to Puteoli. **28:14** There we found some brothers and were invited to stay with them seven days. And in this way we came to Rome. **28:15** The brothers from there, when they heard about us, came as far as the Forum of Appius and Three Taverns to meet us. When he saw them, Paul thanked God and took courage. **28:16** When we entered Rome, Paul was allowed to live by himself, with the soldier who was guarding him.

**28:17** After three days Paul called the local Jewish leaders together. When they had assembled, he said to them, "Brothers, although I had done nothing against our people or the customs of our ancestors, from Jerusalem I was handed over as a prisoner to the Romans. **28:18** When they had heard my case, they wanted to release me, because there was no basis for a death sentence against me. **28:19** But when the Jews objected, I was forced to appeal to Caesar—not that I had some charge to bring against my own people. **28:20** So for this reason I have asked to see you and speak with you, for I am bound with this chain because of the hope of Israel." **28:21** They replied, "We have received no letters from Judea about you, nor have any of the brothers come from there and reported or said anything bad about you. **28:22** But we would like to hear from you what you think, for regarding this sect we know that people everywhere speak against it."

**28:23** They set a day to meet with him, and they came to him where he was staying in even greater numbers. From morning until evening he explained things to them, testifying about the kingdom of God and trying to convince them about Jesus from both the law of Moses and the prophets. **28:24** Some were convinced by what he said, but others refused to believe. **28:25** So they began to leave, unable to agree among themselves, after Paul made one last statement: "The Holy Spirit spoke rightly to your ancestors through the prophet Isaiah **28:26** when he said,

'Go to this people and say,

"You will keep on hearing, but will never understand,

and you will keep on looking, but will never perceive.

**28:27** For the heart of this people has become dull,

and their ears are hard of hearing,

and they have closed their eyes,

so that they would not see with their eyes

and hear with their ears

and understand with their heart

and turn, and I would heal them.""'

**28:28** "Therefore be advised that this salvation from God has been sent to the Gentiles; they will listen!"

**28:30** Paul lived there two whole years in his own rented quarters and welcomed all who came to him, **28:31** proclaiming the kingdom of God and teaching about the Lord Jesus Christ with complete boldness and without restriction.

1. With the narrative you've just read as a backdrop for understanding, now read carefully the six verses below that are our focus for today. Think of Paul in Rome, awaiting trial before Nero, writing to the Colossians, who are primarily Gentiles.

**Colossians 1:24** Now I rejoice in my sufferings for you, and I fill up in my physical body—for the sake of his body, the church—what is lacking in the sufferings of Christ. **1:25** I became a servant of the church according to the stewardship from God—given to me for you—in order to complete the word of God, **1:26** that is, the mystery that has been kept hidden from ages and generations, but has now been revealed to his saints. **1:27** God wanted to make known to them the glorious riches of this mystery among the Gentiles, which is Christ in you, the hope of glory. **1:28** We proclaim him by instructing and teaching all people with all wisdom so that we may present every person mature in Christ. **1:29** Toward this goal I also labor, struggling according to his power that powerfully works in me.

2. According to Acts, why was Paul in Rome? What did it have to do with his ministry of taking the gospel the Gentiles?

_____

_____

_____

3. Note how Paul describes his ministry in other places.

**Acts 13:46** Both Paul and Barnabas replied courageously, "It was necessary to speak the word of God to you [the Jews] first. Since you reject it and do not consider yourselves worthy of eternal life, we are turning to the Gentiles.

**Acts 15:12** The whole group [of elders in Jerusalem] kept quiet and listened to Barnabas and Paul while they explained all the miraculous signs and wonders God had done among the Gentiles through them.

**Acts 21:19** When Paul had greeted [James and the elders], he began to explain in detail what God had done among the Gentiles through his ministry.

**Ephesians 3:1–3** For this reason I, Paul, the prisoner of Christ Jesus for the sake of you Gentiles—if indeed you have heard of the stewardship of God's grace that was given to me for you, that by revelation the divine secret was made known to me, as I wrote before briefly.

4. Keep in mind that the letter going to Ephesians was probably sent in the same pouch as the one for Colossae. According to Ephesians 3:1–3, on what people group is Paul focused?

_____

• *Rejoice in sufferings.* As the story goes, the aging Renoir was asked why he continued to paint when he was in so much pain. His answer: "The pain passes, but the glory remains." That's true even more so of the Christian life. Paul rejoices because his suffering "for you" (Col.

1:24), probably meaning "you Gentiles," completes what was lacking in Christ's sufferings. We'll consider what that means on Saturday.

5. Have you ever made sacrifices for the gospel? If so, what did they cost you? If not, why not?

_____

_____

• *Stewardship.* What's a stewardship? It's a responsibility someone has for something without possessing it, or being the manager but not the owner. Paul says he was given a stewardship, apparently to "complete the Word of God" by revealing to the Gentiles what had previously been a secret: they could have the living God of the universe dwelling inside of them—"Christ in you, the hope of glory."

Years ago, when my husband was in graduate school, to help make ends meet we house-sat for some of Dallas's wealthiest families. Some let us drive their convertibles, soak in their spas, and eat enchiladas prepared by their cooks. Paupers that we were, we loved that part of our job! We took care of other people's pools (by hanging out in them) without having to pay their bills. In short, we had a stewardship—a responsibility (make the place look lived in; maybe feed the dog) without possession.

Yet sometimes people's kids came with the stuff. And even though we were experienced youth workers, we got our first gray hairs from some of those young people. One weekend a high-school girl announced she was going camping with the boys' baseball team and sped off in her classic Mustang. When we called her dad, he tracked her down at the campsite through a park ranger. She returned home several hours later and handed us her keys.

Another weekend a tenth-grade boy slipped out of his second-story bedroom window, stole his big brother's car, and disappeared for the night. We didn't even know he was gone until his parents called from their cruise to tell him good-night, and we went to call him to the phone. We found the room empty and the window open. Nothing takes the thrill from mansion living quite like having parents regale you for losing their kids.

Some stewardships are relatively easy; others can be quite stressful. Paul's was the weightiest of all—"to complete the Word of God." Up to this point, God chose to have a special relationship with the nation of Israel as part of his redemptive plan for all humanity; through the Cross, that relational focus extended from the one people group to the entire world. And God charged Paul with the job of getting the word out at a time when nobody had ever heard of radios, television, mail service, or text messaging.

6. God says even the believer's body is not his or her our own, because we have been bought with a price (1 Cor. 6:19–20). Your body, then, is a stewardship from God. For what else have you been given stewardship—both materially and spiritually?

_____

_____

• *Mystery.* We think of a mystery as a who-done-it with suspense that keeps us from doing the laundry until we know how the story turns out. Yet Paul had in mind a different sort of mystery. When he speaks of mystery, he means something that has never before been known, something that has been hidden in all generations, but is now being revealed. Many people in Colossae believed the way to spiritual vitality was to be part of some inner circle in a mystery religion. To their system of thinking, God was accessible only to a select few.

7. Paul takes the Colossians' word *mystery* and infuses it with gospel meaning. This mystery is not hidden but revealed. This God is wholly accessible, making Himself known to all who desire to know the truth. How did He reveal the truth of the gospel to you?

_____

_____

8. What terms does Paul use to describe the mystery (1:27)?

_____

_____

9. What exactly is the mystery that is now revealed (1:27)?

_____

_____

_____

10. What is Paul's goal in sharing the mystery (1:28)?

_____

_____

_____

11. Paul has resurrection power as he labors toward the goal. Does that mean it's easy for him (1:29)?

_____

_____

12. To whom can you reveal the mystery? How?

_____

_____

## WEDNESDAY: WHAT AN APOSTLE WANTS

1. Read today's text from Colossians. It's short.

> **2:1** For I want you to know how great a struggle I have for you, and for those in Laodicea, and for those who have not met me face to face.

2. See the map of the ancient Mediterranean world on the next page. The distance from Ephesus to Colossae is about 120 miles. Would you say Laodicea is close to or far from Colossae?

Notice in verse 1 that Paul mentions "those in Laodicea." Later in Colossians he mentions the Laodiceans again: "After this letter has been read to you, see that it is also read in the church of the Laodiceans and that you in turn read the letter from Laodicea" (4:16, NIV).

Some scholars, including many conservatives, believe that Paul's letter to the Ephesians actually went to Laodicea first. The book of Ephesians begins, "From Paul, an apostle of Christ Jesus by the will of God, to the saints, the faithful in Christ Jesus" (1:1). Later manuscripts added the words *in Ephesus* after the word *saints*, but the earliest, most important manuscripts didn't include this phrase. Also of note is that a second-century theologian named Marcion composed a list of Paul's epistles, and that list included a "letter to the Laodiceans." This letter was likely the letter we know today as Ephesians.

The fact that Ephesians includes no greetings to individuals provides another hint that the book was intended as a circulating letter, written to be read in churches throughout the area. Paul lived in Ephesus for three years and knew many people there, but he knew no one in Laodicea.

Look at the map again. Tychicus, traveling to Colossae from Rome (from the west), would have first landed at the port of Ephesus. From there he probably would have gone inland to Laodicea and then on to Colossae. Paul may have left in his letter a fill-in-the-blank space for each church to complete for public reading (sort of like some do today with form-letter document/merge files). This would account for some manuscripts having *Ephesus*, the earliest manuscripts having nothing at all, and Marcion's listing of Paul's "letter to the Laodiceans."

All such minor variants in the copies of original Bible documents are just that—minor.[6] None of them occur in areas of core doctrines. Phrases such as "He is the image of the invisible God" are never in question!

3. Paul expected his readers to share the two letters. Pray for spiritual insight and then read what we know as the book of Ephesians. Highlight themes that seem familiar compared with what you read in Colossians. Words in underlined italic are the apostle's quotations from the Old Testament.

### Ephesians 1

**1:1** From Paul, an apostle of Christ Jesus by the will of God, to the saints [in Ephesus], the faithful in Christ Jesus. **1:2** Grace and peace to you from God our Father and the Lord Jesus Christ!

**1:3** Blessed is the God and Father of our Lord Jesus Christ, who has blessed us with every spiritual blessing in the heavenly realms in Christ. **1:4** For he chose us in Christ before the foundation of the world that we may be holy and unblemished in his sight in love. **1:5** He did this by predestining us to adoption as his sons through Jesus Christ, according to the pleasure of his will—**1:6** to the praise of the glory of his grace that he has freely bestowed on us in his dearly loved Son. **1:7** In him we have redemption through his blood, the forgiveness of our trespasses, according to the riches of his grace **1:8** that he lavished on us in all wisdom and insight. **1:9** He did this when he revealed to us the secret of his will, according to his good pleasure that he set forth in Christ, **1:10** toward the administration of the fullness of the times, to head up all things in Christ—the things in heaven and the things on earth. **1:11** In Christ we too have been claimed as God's own possession, since we were predestined according to the one purpose of him who accomplishes all things according to the counsel of his will **1:12** so that we, who were the first to set our hope on Christ, would be to the praise of his glory. **1:13** And when you heard the word of truth (the gospel of your salvation)—when you believed in Christ—you were marked with the seal of the promised Holy Spirit, **1:14** who is the down payment of our inheritance, until the redemption of God's own possession, to the praise of his glory.

**1:15** For this reason, because I have heard of your faith in the Lord Jesus and your love for all the saints, **1:16** I do not cease to give

[6] For a thorough analysis of such minor variations, read *Reinventing Jesus* by Komoszewski and Wallace

thanks for you when I remember you in my prayers. **1:17** I pray that the God of our Lord Jesus Christ, the Father of glory, may give you spiritual wisdom and revelation in your growing knowledge of him, **1:18**— since the eyes of your heart have been enlightened—so that you may know what is the hope of his calling, what is the wealth of his glorious inheritance in the saints, **1:19** and what is the incomparable greatness of his power toward us who believe, as displayed in the exercise of his immense strength. **1:20** This power he exercised in Christ when he raised him from the dead and seated him at his right hand in the heavenly realms **1:21** far above every rule and authority and power and dominion and every name that is named, not only in this age but also in the one to come. **1:22** And God put all things under Christ's feet, and he gave him to the church as head over all things. **1:23** Now the church is his body, the fullness of him who fills all in all.

## Ephesians 2

**2:1** And although you were dead in your transgressions and sins, **2:2** in which you formerly lived according to this world's present path, according to the ruler of the kingdom of the air, the ruler of the spirit that is now energizing the sons of disobedience, **2:3** among whom all of us also formerly lived out our lives in the cravings of our flesh, indulging the desires of the flesh and the mind, and were by nature children of wrath even as the rest...

**2:4** But God, being rich in mercy, because of his great love with which he loved us, **2:5** even though we were dead in transgressions, made us alive together with Christ—by grace you are saved!—**2:6** and he raised us up with him and seated us with him in the heavenly realms in Christ Jesus, **2:7** to demonstrate in the coming ages the surpassing wealth of his grace in kindness toward us in Christ Jesus. **2:8** For by grace you are saved through faith, and this is not from yourselves, it is the gift of God; **2:9** it is not from works, so that no one can boast. **2:10** For we are his workmanship, having been created in Christ Jesus for good works that God prepared beforehand so we may do them.

**2:11** Therefore remember that formerly you, the Gentiles in the flesh—who are called "uncircumcision" by the so-called "circumcision" that is performed on the body by human hands—**2:12** that you were at that time without the Messiah, alienated from the citizenship of Israel and strangers to the covenants of promise, having no hope and without God in the world. **2:13** But now in Christ Jesus you who used to be far away have been brought near by the blood of Christ. **2:14** For he is our peace, the one who made both groups into one and who destroyed the middle wall of partition, the hostility, **2:15** when he nullified in his flesh the law of commandments in decrees. He did this to create in himself one new man out of two, thus making peace, **2:16** and to reconcile them both in one body to God through the cross, by which the hostility has been killed. **2:17** And he came and preached peace to you who were far off and peace to those who were near, **2:18** so that through him we both have access in one Spirit to the Father. **2:19** So then you are no longer foreigners and noncitizens, but you are fellow citizens with the saints and members of God's household, **2:20** because you have been built on the foundation of the apostles and prophets, with Christ Jesus himself as the cornerstone. **2:21** In him the whole building, being joined together, grows into a holy temple in the Lord, **2:22** in whom you also are being built together into a dwelling place of God in the Spirit.

### Ephesians 3

**3:1** For this reason I, Paul, the prisoner of Christ Jesus for the sake of you Gentiles—**3:2** if indeed you have heard of the stewardship of God's grace that was given to me for you, **3:3** that by revelation the divine secret was made known to me, as I wrote before briefly. **3:4** When reading this, you will be able to understand my insight into this secret of Christ. **3:5** Now this secret was not disclosed to people in former generations as it has now been revealed to his holy apostles and prophets by the Spirit, **3:6** namely, that through the gospel the Gentiles are fellow heirs, fellow members of the body, and fellow partakers of the promise in Christ Jesus. **3:7** I became a servant of this gospel according to the gift of God's grace that was given to me by the exercise of his power. **3:8** To me—less than the least of all the saints—this grace was given, to proclaim to the Gentiles the unfathomable riches of Christ **3:9** and to enlighten everyone about God's secret plan—a secret that has been hidden for ages in God who has created all things. **3:10** The purpose of this enlightenment is that through the church the multifaceted wisdom of God should now be disclosed to the rulers and the authorities in the heavenly realms. **3:11** This was according to the eternal purpose that he accomplished in Christ Jesus our Lord, **3:12** in whom we have boldness and confident access to God because of Christ's faithfulness. **3:13** For this reason I ask you not to lose heart because of what I am suffering for you, which is your glory.

**3:14** For this reason I kneel before the Father, **3:15** from whom every family in heaven and on the earth is named. **3:16** I pray that according to the wealth of his glory he may grant you to be strengthened with power through his Spirit in the inner person, **3:17** that Christ may dwell in your hearts through faith, so that, because you have been rooted and grounded in love, **3:18** you may be able to comprehend with all the saints what is the breadth and length and height and depth, **3:19** and thus to know the love of Christ that surpasses knowledge, so that you may be filled up to all the fullness of God.

**3:20** Now to him who by the power that is working within us is able to do far beyond all that we ask or think, **3:21** to him be the glory in the church and in Christ Jesus to all generations, forever and ever. Amen.

## Ephesians 4

**4:1** I, therefore, the prisoner for the Lord, urge you to live worthily of the calling with which you have been called, **4:2** with all humility and gentleness, with patience, bearing with one another in love, **4:3** making every effort to keep the unity of the Spirit in the bond of peace. **4:4** There is one body and one Spirit, just as you too were called to the one hope of your calling, **4:5** one Lord, one faith, one baptism, **4:6** one God and Father of all, who is over all and through all and in all.

**4:7** But to each one of us grace was given according to the measure of the gift of Christ. **4:8** Therefore it says, _"When he ascended on high he captured captives; he gave gifts to men."_ **4:9** Now what is the meaning of _"he ascended,"_ except that he also descended to the lower regions, namely, the earth? **4:10** He, the very one who descended, is also the one who ascended above all the heavens, in order to fill all things. **4:11** It was he who gave some as apostles, some as prophets, some as evangelists, and some as pastors and teachers, **4:12** to equip the saints for the work of ministry, that is, to build up the body of Christ, **4:13** until we all attain to the unity of the faith and of the knowledge of the Son of God—a mature person, attaining to the measure of Christ's full stature. **4:14** So we are no longer to be children, tossed back and forth by waves and carried about by every wind of teaching by the trickery of people who craftily carry out their deceitful schemes. **4:15** But practicing the truth in love, we will in all things grow up into Christ, who is the head. **4:16** From him the whole body grows, fitted and held together through every supporting ligament. As each one does its part, the body grows in love.

**4:17** So I say this, and insist in the Lord, that you no longer live as the Gentiles do, in the futility of their thinking. **4:18** They are darkened in their understanding, being alienated from the life of God because of the ignorance that is in them due to the hardness of their hearts. **4:19** Because they are callous, they have given themselves over to indecency for the practice of every kind of impurity with greediness. **4:20** But you did not learn about Christ like this, **4:21** if indeed you heard about him and were taught in him, just as the truth is in Jesus. **4:22** You were taught with reference to your former way of life to lay aside the old man who is being corrupted in accordance with deceitful desires, **4:23** to be renewed in the spirit of your mind, **4:24** and to put on the new man who has been created in God's image—in righteousness and holiness that comes from truth.

**4:25** Therefore, having laid aside falsehood, _each one of you speak the truth with his neighbor,_ for we are members of one another. **4:26** _Be angry and do not sin;_ do not let the sun go down on the cause of your anger. **4:27** Do not give the devil an opportunity. **4:28** The one who steals must steal no longer; rather he must labor, doing good with his own hands, so that he may have something to share with the one who has need. **4:29** You must let no unwholesome word come out of your mouth, but only what is beneficial for the building up of the one in need, that it may give grace to those who hear. **4:30** And do not grieve the Holy Spirit of God, by whom you were sealed for the day of redemption. **4:31** You must put away every kind of bitterness, anger, wrath, quarreling, and evil, slanderous talk. **4:32** Instead, be kind to one another, compassionate, forgiving one another, just as God in Christ also forgave you.

## Ephesians 5

**5:1** Therefore, be imitators of God as dearly loved children **5:2** and live in love, just as Christ also loved us and gave himself for us, a sacrificial and fragrant offering to God. **5:3** But among you there must not be either sexual immorality, impurity of any kind, or greed, as these are not fitting for the saints. **5:4** Neither should there be vulgar speech, foolish talk, or coarse jesting—all of which are out of character—but rather thanksgiving. **5:5** For you can be confident of this one thing: that no person who is immoral, impure, or greedy (such a person is an idolater) has any inheritance in the kingdom of Christ and God.

**5:6** Let nobody deceive you with empty words, for because of these things God's wrath comes on the sons of disobedience. **5:7** Therefore do not be partakers with them, **5:8** for you were at one time darkness, but now you are light in the Lord. Walk as children of the light—**5:9** for the fruit of the light consists in all goodness, righteousness, and truth—**5:10** trying to learn what is pleasing to the Lord. **5:11** Do not participate in the unfruitful deeds of darkness, but rather expose them. **5:12** For the things they do in secret are shameful even to mention. **5:13** But all things being exposed by the light are made evident. **5:14** For everything made evident is light, and for this reason it says:

"Awake, O sleeper!

Rise from the dead,

and Christ will shine on you!"

**5:15** Therefore be very careful how you live—not as unwise but as wise, **5:16** taking advantage of every opportunity, because the days are evil. **5:17** For this reason do not be foolish, but be wise by understanding what the Lord's will is. **5:18** And do not get drunk with wine, which is debauchery, but be filled by the Spirit, **5:19** speaking to one another in psalms, hymns, and spiritual songs, singing and making music in your hearts to the Lord, **5:20** always giving thanks to God the Father for each other in the name of our Lord Jesus Christ, **5:21** and submitting to one another out of reverence for Christ.

**5:22** Wives, submit to your husbands as to the Lord, **5:23** because the husband is the head of the wife as also Christ is the head of the church—he himself being the savior of the body. **5:24** But as the church submits to Christ, so also wives should submit to their husbands in everything. **5:25** Husbands, love your wives just as Christ loved the church and gave himself for her **5:26** to sanctify her by cleansing her with the washing of the water by the word, **5:27** so that he may present the church to himself as glorious—not having a stain or wrinkle, or any such blemish, but holy and blameless. **5:28** In the same way husbands ought to love their wives as their own bodies. He who loves his wife loves himself. **5:29** For no one has ever hated his own body but he feeds it and takes care of it, just as Christ also does the church, **5:30** for we are members of his body. **5:31** _For this reason a man will leave his father and mother and will be joined to his wife, and the two will become one flesh._ **5:32** This mystery is great—but I am actually speaking with reference to Christ and the church. **5:33** Nevertheless, each one of you must also love his own wife as he loves himself, and the wife must respect her husband.

## Ephesians 6

**6:1** Children, obey your parents in the Lord for this is right. **6:2** "_Honor your father and mother,_" which is the first commandment accompanied by a promise, namely, **6:3** _"that it may go well with you and that you will live a long time on the earth."_

**6:4** Fathers, do not provoke your children to anger, but raise them up in the discipline and instruction of the Lord.

**6:5** Slaves, obey your human masters with fear and trembling, in the sincerity of your heart as to Christ, **6:6** not like those who do their work only when someone is watching—as people-pleasers—but as slaves of Christ doing the will of God from the heart. **6:7** Obey with enthusiasm, as though serving the Lord and not people, **6:8** because you know that each person, whether slave or free, if he does something good, this will be rewarded by the Lord.

**6:9** Masters, treat your slaves the same way, giving up the use of threats, because you know that both you and they have the same master in heaven, and there is no favoritism with him.

**6:10** Finally, be strengthened in the Lord and in the strength of his power. **6:11** Clothe yourselves with the full armor of God so that you may be able to stand against the schemes of the devil. **6:12** For our struggle is not against flesh and blood, but against the rulers, against the powers, against the world rulers of this darkness, against the spiritual forces of evil in the heavens. **6:13** For this reason, take up the full armor of God so that you may be able to stand your ground on the evil day, and having done everything, to stand. **6:14** Stand firm therefore, by fastening the belt of truth around your waist, by putting on the breastplate of righteousness, **6:15** by fitting your feet with the preparation that comes from the good news of peace, **6:16** and in all of this, by taking up the shield of faith with which you can extinguish all the flaming arrows of the evil one. **6:17** And take _the helmet of salvation_ and the sword of the Spirit, which is the word of God. **6:18** With every prayer and petition, pray at all times in the Spirit, and to this end be alert, with all perseverance and requests for all the saints. **6:19** Pray for me also, that I may be given the message when I begin to speak—that I may confidently make known the mystery of the gospel, **6:20** for which I am an ambassador in chains. Pray that I may be able to speak boldly as I ought to speak.

**6:21** Tychicus, my dear brother and faithful servant in the Lord, will make everything known to you, so that you too may know about my circumstances, how I am doing. **6:22** I have sent him to you for this very purpose, that you may know our circumstances and that he may encourage your hearts.

**6:23** Peace to the brothers and sisters, and love with faith, from God the Father and the Lord Jesus Christ. **6:24** Grace be with all of those who love our Lord Jesus Christ with an undying love.

4. What ideas or topics overlap in this document with what Paul wrote to the Colossians?

_____

_____

5. Considering what Paul wrote in both books, summarize what you think he wants to emphasize for his readers in this part of the world.

_____

_____

_____

6. As you read, what commandments did you encounter that you need to obey?

_____

_____

_____

_____

## Thursday: The Letter

1. Pray for the Holy Spirit to help you understand; then read Colossians 2:2–7.

> **2:2** My goal is that their hearts, having been knit together in love, may be encouraged, and that they may have all the riches that assurance brings in their understanding of the knowledge of the mystery of God, namely, Christ, **2:3** in whom are hidden all the treasures of wisdom and knowledge. **2:4** I say this so that no one will deceive you through arguments that sound reasonable. **2:5** For though I am absent from you in body, I am present with you in spirit, rejoicing to see your morale and the firmness of your faith in

Christ.

**2:6** Therefore, just as you received Christ Jesus as Lord, continue to live your lives in him, **2:7** rooted and built up in him and firm in your faith just as you were taught, and overflowing with thankfulness.

2. Paul writes, "For I want you to know how great a struggle I have for you, and for those in Laodicea, and for those who have not met me face to face" (2:1). Why do you think he's struggling for people he does not even know? Why does he care about them?

_____

_____

_____

3. What is Paul's goal for his readers (2:2)?

_____

_____

_____

4. Though Paul wrote this to a church about two thousand years ago, believers today are still members of the body of Christ. So what was important for the Colossians' faith is important for ours too. Is your heart "knit together in love" with other believers? Do you give and receive encouragement with other believers? Why or why not?

_____

_____

_____

5. Why would assurance be important to our understanding of the knowledge of God?

_____

_____

_____

6. According to Colossians 2:2, what is the mystery of God?

_____

7. Gnosticism was not yet fully formed when Paul wrote to the Colossians, but it existed. Gnostic thought says that only a select few are privy to secret spiritual mysteries. It also deemphasizes flesh and emphasizes spirit only. (Such thinking leads to anti-sex and anti-physician sorts of applications, as one elevates spirit over flesh.) How does Colossians 2:2–4 address such thinking?

_____

_____

_____

_____

8. In Colossians 2:6 the word *as* appears. Paul is noting two parallels. What is his exhortation (2:6)?

_____

_____

_____

9. Paul affirms that his readers have started well—receiving Christ Jesus as Lord and living in Him. He wants them to continue doing so. He probably has in mind Psalm 1, which includes an extended metaphor about the righteous person being like a tree planted by rivers and bringing forth fruit. So picture a tree growing. What do you think it means to be the following (v. 7)?

- rooted in Him?

_____

_____

- built up in Him?

_____

_____

- firm in your faith as you were taught?

_____

_____

- overflowing with thankfulness?

_____

_____

10. Are you rooted in Him? Built up in Him? Firm in your faith? What steps can you take to become more grounded?

_____

_____

_____

11. Overflowing with thankfulness means being consciously and constantly aware of God's blessings. Make a list of things for which you're thankful. Use a separate piece of paper if you need more space—which you probably will. Pray as you write, expressing gratitude to God for what He's done for you physically, relationally, emotionally, and spiritually.

## FRIDAY: IN THE BEGINNING

1. Prayerfully read Colossians 2:8–23.

**2:8** Be careful not to allow anyone to captivate you through an empty, deceitful philosophy that is according to human traditions and the elemental spirits of the world, and not according to Christ. **2:9** For in him all the fullness of deity lives in bodily form, **2:10** and you have been filled in him, who is the head over every ruler and authority.

**2:11** In him you also were circumcised—not, however, with a circumcision performed by human hands, but by the removal of the fleshly body, that is, through the circumcision done by Christ. **2:12** Having been buried with him in baptism, you also have been raised with him through your faith in the power of God who raised him from the dead. **2:13** And even though you were dead in your transgressions and in the uncircumcision of your flesh, he nevertheless made you alive with him, having forgiven all your transgressions. **2:14** He has destroyed what was against us, a certificate of indebtedness expressed in decrees opposed to us. He has taken it away by nailing it to the cross. **2:15** Disarming the rulers and authorities, he has made a public disgrace of them, triumphing over them by the cross.

**2:16** Therefore do not let anyone judge you with respect to food or drink, or in the matter of a feast, new moon, or Sabbath days—**2:17** these are only the shadow of the things to come, but the reality is Christ! **2:18** Let no one who delights in humility and the worship of angels pass judgment on you. That person goes on at great lengths about what he has supposedly seen, but he is puffed up with empty notions by his fleshly mind. **2:19** He has not held fast to the head from whom the whole body, supported and knit together through its ligaments and sinews, grows with a growth that is from God.

**2:20** If you have died with Christ to the elemental spirits of the world, why do you submit to them as though you lived in the world? **2:21** "Do not handle! Do not taste! Do not touch!" **2:22** These are all destined to perish with use, founded as they are on human commands and teachings. **2:23** Even though they have the appearance of wisdom with their self-imposed worship and false humility achieved by an unsparing treatment of the body—a wisdom with no true value—they in reality result in fleshly indulgence.

2. In Colossians 2:9–10 and 2:18–19, Paul uses an extended metaphor of a head and body. Underline all words or phrases having to do with a physical body:

> **Colossians 2:9** For in him all the fullness of deity lives in bodily form, **2:10** and you have been filled in him, who is the head over every ruler and authority.
>
> **2:18** Let no one who delights in humility and the worship of angels pass judgment on you. That person goes on at great lengths about what he has supposedly seen, but he is puffed up with empty notions by his fleshly mind. **2:19** He has not held fast to the head from whom the whole body, supported and knit together through its ligaments and sinews, grows with a growth that is from God.

3. Paul uses the idea of fullness two ways in verses 9–10. What does he say about God's fullness? What does he say about the believer's fullness?

_____

_____

_____

• *Head.* Most often in Greek, as in English, the word *head* is used of a body part—a literal head, the kind that's attached to the neck. Paul's favorite metaphor for the church is that of a body connected to its head, Christ. Words and phrases that relate to physical bodies show up whenever he uses it this way: "knit together" and "grows" (2:19) and "every supporting ligament" and "builds itself up" (Eph. 4:16, NIV). The head/body connection emphasizes our oneness with Him and our process of maturing in Him.

Paul's favorite metaphor for marriage is a body (wife) connected to a head (husband) (see Eph. 5:21–33). Again, it is a unity picture, an image that communicates two becoming one.

In Colossians 2, note Paul's wording about what the head does: serves as the source through which the body is supported, knitted, and grown. It's an organic picture, one of interconnection. Here he speaks of a mystery revealed. He tells of another "mystery now revealed" over in Ephesians (5:32)—that marriage pictures the relationship between Christ and the church. Again, Paul chooses to illustrate using a head/body connection.

A secondary use of *head* in Greek is the idea of being first. As we considered last week, this use is what Paul seems to have had in mind in Colossians 2:10 ("head over every ruler and authority"). Notice that in this analogy, there is not a body anywhere except the human form he fills. Notice too the different prepositions—*over* and *of*—that we use in English to show the difference in meaning. A head over authority brings to mind an organization chart with a clearly defined hierarchy, but the head of a human attached to a body emphasizes interconnectedness.

The idea of being first here fits with Paul's emphasis on Jesus being firstborn (1:15, 18). Paul uses other words that relate to "firstness" as well. Notice how he talks of "elemental spirits of the world" (2:8). The word for *elemental* is connected with firsts and beginnings. In grammar, the elements are the ABCs; in philosophy, the axioms; in the material world, the basic elements. Jesus Christ as firstborn is Authority of authorities, Ruler of rulers, First of firsts.

• *Circumcision.* In Genesis 17:10, we read that God made a covenant with Abraham, and as part of that covenant He told Abraham to circumcise all of his male descendants. Circumcision is the removal of the prepuce, or foreskin, the fold of skin that covers the head of the penis. While pagans in the ancient Near East incorporated sexual immorality into much of their worship, those who were circumcised bore on their most personal part the sign that they belonged to Yahweh, the self-existing one.

My husband and I were sitting in a high school Sunday school class one morning when one of the students got up and announced, "The youth pastor circumcised me to lead in prayer this morning." There was a stunned silence; then everyone burst into uncontrollable laughter. He had meant to say, "He christened me to lead. . . . "

After that faux pas, some of the visitors wanted to know what circumcision was. What made those high school students laugh is that it's kind of personal and thus embarrassing. Actually, it's not kind of personal, it's super-personal. God intended circumcision to be more than just a physical act, though. In Deuteronomy 10:16, 30:6, and Jeremiah 4:4, we find literal circumcision used as a metaphor. God reveals the ideal: circumcision of the heart, to be set apart for God on the inside in addition to the outside. In Colossians, Paul tells the Gentile Christians, who were not part of the original Abrahamic covenant, that they have been circumcised, or marked out, as God's because of the work of Christ.

4. Highlight or circle every time a form of the word *circumcision* appears.

> **Colossians 2:11** In him you also were circumcised—not, however, with a circumcision performed by human hands, but by the removal of the fleshly body, that is, through the circumcision done by Christ. **2:12** Having been buried with him in baptism, you also have been raised with him through your faith in the power of God who raised him from the dead. **2:13** And even though you were dead in your transgressions and in the uncircumcision of your flesh, he nevertheless made you alive with him, having forgiven all your transgressions. **2:14** He has destroyed what was against us, a certificate of indebtedness expressed in decrees opposed to us. He has taken it away by nailing it to the cross. **2:15** Disarming the rulers and authorities, he has made a public disgrace of them, triumphing over them by the cross.

5. Summarize what you think Paul is saying to these Gentiles in Colossians 2:11–15.

_____

_____

_____

• *Therefore.* "Consequently, as a result." Because of Jesus' finished work on the cross that has given Gentiles spiritual benefits, Paul gives some commands.

> **Colossians 2:16** Therefore do not let anyone judge you with respect to food or drink, or in the matter of a feast, new moon, or

Sabbath days—**2:17** these are only the shadow of the things to come, but the reality is Christ!

**2:18** Let no one who delights in humility and the worship of angels pass judgment on you. That person goes on at great lengths about what he has supposedly seen, but he is puffed up with empty notions by his fleshly mind. **2:19** He has not held fast to the head from whom the whole body, supported and knit together through its ligaments and sinews, grows with a growth that is from God.

**2:20** If you have died with Christ to the elemental spirits of the world, why do you submit to them as though you lived in the world? **2:21** "Do not handle! Do not taste! Do not touch!" **2:22** These are all destined to perish with use, founded as they are on human commands and teachings. **2:23** Even though they have the appearance of wisdom with their self-imposed worship and false humility achieved by an unsparing treatment of the body—a wisdom with no true value—they in reality result in fleshly indulgence.

6. For what are the Colossian Christians not to allow anyone to judge them (2:16, 18)?

_____

_____

Picture a group of observant Jews. They're circumcised. They observe Passover, the Feasts of Unleavened Bread and Pentecost, the Day of Atonement, the Feast of Tabernacles. They don't eat pork and a lot of other prohibited foods. At the time of every new moon, approximately once a month, they bring a burnt offering to God. And every Friday through Saturday, sundown to sundown, all their labor screeches to a halt. They have other holidays too—sabbaths in addition to the weekly one.

Next, share the gospel of Jesus Christ with members of this group, showing them how Christ foreshadowed and fulfilled all their practices. Rejoice when some come to faith; weep when others reject the good news.

Next, share the gospel with a bunch of Gentiles. Rejoice when some of them come to faith too! Teach them all to focus on knowing and following Jesus.

Then watch as the Jewish believers judge the non-Jews, saying,

"Why aren't you circumcised? Why aren't you observing the Passover? Why do you eat pork? Where were you when we made the new moon sacrifice?" The Jewish Christians look down on the Gentile believers for being unobservant and insist that to be right with God, the Gentiles must keep the Law of Moses.

To complicate matters, some of the Gentiles have been duped by the prevailing philosophy that says matter is evil. Proponents of this philosophy conclude that a holy God could not have made the material world—that only what is spiritual is sacred. They say that a long series of demigod offshoots proceeded from God and that once the generations got far enough removed from the original in the evolutionary process, one of the demigods could stoop so low as to create matter. These proto-Gnostics would say, "We are not good enough to come directly to God. But we can start with the angels, which, if we are in correct spirit, will elevate our requests through the hierarchy to God. And if you're really spiritual, you'll get to have one of these angel encounters and get in on the secret stuff from God."

Paul has a message for the believers getting hit from both sides: Don't let anybody judge you about these things!

7. What reason does Paul give for the Gentiles refusing to let themselves be judged (2:17, 22)?

_____

_____

8. One of my professors once placed his hand on the glass of an overhead projector and turned on the light, projecting an image of his hand onto the screen. Then he asked us which was better—the shadow of his hand or the hand itself. How does a shadow relate to what is real and solid? Why do you think shadow is a fitting image for Paul to use when addressing those who look down on matter?

_____

_____

_____

9. One thing that sets apart Christianity from other philosophies is the concept of grace. Another is the presentation of both matter and spirit as being from God. What do the facts that Christ created all (both visible and invisible) and that God took on human flesh say to those who rank matter over spirit or vice versa?

_____

_____

10. Give thanks for the fact that you live in a time when practices that foreshadowed the arrival of Christ have been fulfilled in your wonderful Savior. List some of your spiritual benefits; then spend time giving thanks for them.

_____

_____

_____

11. With whom can you share "Christ in you—the hope of glory"?

_____

## SATURDAY: SOMETHING LACKING?

**Scripture:** "Now I rejoice in my sufferings for you, and I fill up in my physical body—for the sake of his body, the church—what is lacking in the sufferings of Christ." (Col. 1:24)

For what are you thankful? I posted the question on my blog shortly after Thanksgiving with the promise that the person with the most unexpected or unusual comment would win a copy of one of my Bible studies to keep or re-gift as a Christmas present. Here is a sampling of the answers I received:

Reiko said: "I am thankful that my husband has been unemployed for the last eight months, and our family's faith has developed, and our relationships have deepened in the process. I am also thankful that

God will also provide my husband a job soon. I am thankful for my friends from church, who have been praying for us as well."

Erin said: "I'm thankful that *in-laws* is not a word that makes me cringe. Though I come from a very different background than my husband, his family has always welcomed me with open arms and encouragement. I actually look forward to being with them through the holidays! (But I don't know if anyone can beat Reiko's 'I'm thankful my husband is unemployed!')"

Amy said: "I'm thankful to be thankful. I've been told that those who've come from where I have become very bitter and really messed up—neither of which I am—or at least I don't think I'm messed up!"

Kelley said: "Yeah, I think Reiko beats us all. . . . I'm thankful for friends who are sad to see me leave our church yet don't set me at an emotional arm's length during the process of leaving. I'm thankful that our house took eighteen months to sell, so many friends at church got to see my daughter born and enjoy her first year."

No surprise—an independent judge found Reiko's entry "most unexpected or unusual." Eight months of unemployment has meant unimaginable hardship for her and her family. The season without work followed their return from Japan, where they served as missionaries. Their present difficulty is related to their choice to spread the gospel. Along with their elementary-age children, they have suffered true want—after serving God! They wonder how they'll keep a roof over their heads, food on the table, and bill collectors away. Yet Reiko rejoices. Her words seem to echo something Paul wrote to the church at Colossae as he was imprisoned in Rome: "Now I rejoice in my sufferings for you, and I fill up in my physical body—for the sake of his body, the church—what is lacking in the sufferings of Christ" (Col. 1:24).

What does it mean to "fill up what is lacking in the sufferings of Christ"? Was the sacrifice of Jesus on the cross somehow insufficient to pay for sins? Surely not! Jesus' utterance "It is finished" was a one-word accounting term for "paid in full." And Paul's choice of the word for *sufferings* in Colossians differs from the one used to describe Jesus' atoning sacrifice (and elsewhere it is used to mean "afflictions").

Numerous volumes have focused on unpacking Paul's verbal luggage in Colossians 1:24. Here's our best guess: While through Jesus' body the once-for-all work of atoning for sin on the cross was finished, the task of spreading the good news to the Gentiles, and the consequential suffering, remained unfinished. Paul, as apostle to the Gentiles, was called to reveal the mystery previously hidden: that God included the Gentiles in His salvation plan. For a Jewish man with Paul's credentials to preach such a thing outraged lots of powerful people! So Paul bore the punishment in his body for taking the gospel to those outside of the house of Israel. Yet he was happy to do so—he rejoiced!—because he had an eternal perspective.

Christ's sufferings on the cross were not lacking in the sense of being flawed; his suffering for sin was finished. But the news of the cross had to spread before the Gentiles could know what had been done on their behalf, and the process of spreading the gospel to the Gentiles required Paul to suffer bodily. Yet he writes to the predominately Gentile believers in Colossae, "I rejoice in my sufferings for you." He suffered for people he'd never met because they had come to faith as the by-product of his preaching the very message that had landed him in a Roman prison.

Though Paul began the work of making known this mystery, many remain unreached. So the task falls to us. Each of us. We are called to make Christ known where He is not yet named. And fulfilling that commission requires sacrifice. It may mean risking unemployment, financial loss, misunderstanding by family members, and persecution—because of the choices we make to follow the one who suffered once for all.

What sacrifices are you willing to make so those who don't know about the glorious riches available in Christ can hear and receive?

**Prayer:** *Gracious heavenly Father, thank You for Your grace. Thank You for sending Your Son to take on human flesh and Your Spirit who indwells all believers. Thank You for extending Your redemptive plan beyond the nation of Israel to the Gentiles. Thank You that we don't have to keep a long list of practices to garner Your favor, but that through our identification with Christ in His death, we can have newness of life. Grant me the courage to take risks in making Your name known and magnified in all the earth. In Jesus' name, Amen.*

**For Memorization:** "For in him all the fullness of deity lives in bodily form, and you have been filled in him, who is the head over every ruler and authority." (Col. 2:9–10)

# Week 3 of 4

## *Christ the Master: Colossians 3:1–4:1*

## SUNDAY: THE OTHER S-WORD

**Scripture:** "Wives, submit to your husbands, as is fitting in the Lord. Husbands, love your wives and do not be embittered against them." (Col. 3:18–19)

For Christmas last year, my husband's brother and his family got a puppy. This year we spent the holidays with them and, being cat people and thus uninitiated in dog ways, we received an introduction to the world of dogdom. At one point, when my brother-in-law arrived home from running errands, the dog got so excited to see him that she peed on the floor. My sister-in-law later told me female dogs will also do that in the presence of an alpha dog as a sign of their submission. Naturally, all sorts of lame jokes ensued about spinning the incontinence problems that accompany age as signs not of bladder weakness but of marital maturity.

It's probably the best-known verse in the Bible: "Wives, submit to your husbands." We find it once in Colossians 3 and twice over in

Ephesians 5. Less quoted is its counterpart, "Husbands, love your wives," which also appears once in Colossians and twice in Ephesians 5.

Do you see a parallel in Paul's thinking? Husbands and wives receive consistent instruction that appears both here and in another epistle Paul probably wrote at the same time to believers in the same part of the empire. And the imperative he chose for wives is *submit*.

If you ask many Christians today, they'll tell you Paul's command to husbands is to head, or lead. They think of the husband as being like the alpha dog, the main marriage partner, the one in charge. But *head* is a noun, and it matches up with the wife's noun—*body*. The counterpart to her verb, *submit*, is his verb, *love*.

In their unique ways, then, both husband and wife are called to self-sacrifice. Many of us, raised on a steady dose of Hollywood, think of love as romance, affection, and feel-good warmth. We even say Paul commanded this kind of love because women have such a great need for affection. As a result, we think, *She obeys; he shows affection.* Yet that is not the kind of love Paul has in mind when he chooses to call husbands to *agape*, to love with the selfless, un-fun kind of love. The hard kind. The kind that looks a lot like giving up your will for another. The kind that looks really similar to submission.

Sadly, a misunderstanding about this biblical marital instruction leads many women to think God is unfair. Believing the Bible teaches that they are the only ones in the marriage whom God calls to give up anything, they envision the female half of marriage devoted to selflessness while the other kicks back and sends her for his drink during the kickoff—all the while assuring himself he's in God's perfect will. And these wives know the odds of a marriage like that working out.

Some at Christian marriage conferences teach that the biblical ideal is for the husband to make the final decisions. The more biblical the marriage, they say, the more such a husband will take the lead. Yet consider the only time in the Bible where we see a married couple given instruction about decision making. It occurs in the context of a couple's most intimate act, and it assumes mature Christians will make decisions mutually, with neither having to make a final decision: "The wife does not have authority over her own body, but the husband does; and likewise also the husband does not have authority over his own body, but the wife does. Stop depriving one another, *except by agreement* for a time, so that you may devote yourselves to prayer, and come together again so that Satan will not tempt you because of your lack of self-control (1 Cor. 7:4–5, NASB, italics mine). The more

Christlike the couple, the more they can make decisions mutually. The goal of marriage is oneness. Two shall become one. A head and a body connect and need each other. Unity rules. Both husband and wife give up their rights for the good of the other.

The submission to which a woman is called differs from obedience. Obedience is what's supposed to happen when a lower-ranking person in a chain of command receives an imperative from a higher-ranking person. We see the word for this used regarding children and slaves. Yet submission is different. It's what happens when two are equal in every way, but one voluntarily places himself or herself under the other. The ultimate example of this is Jesus Christ at His incarnation. Paul wrote in Philippians 2:5–8: "Your attitude should be the same as that of Christ Jesus: Who, being in very nature God, did not consider equality with God something to be grasped, but made himself nothing, taking the very nature of a servant, being made in human likeness. And being found in appearance as a man, he humbled himself and became obedient to death—even death on a cross!" (NIV).

The Son is equal with the Father, yet He chose to place Himself under the Father. Wives are equal with their husbands, yet they voluntarily place themselves under them.

So the wife is to submit and the husband is to sacrifice. An argument in such a home should look something like this:

"I insist that you have your way."

"No, no, really, I insist you have your way."

The whole alpha male/submissive female idea works in the world of dogdom, but in marriage it distorts the unity picture Paul envisioned. There is only one Alpha in a union of two Christ-followers. In fact, He's the Alpha and Omega. The ultimate modeler of submission in His earthly sojourn, He is the one who holds the universe—and all things, including relationships—together.

## MONDAY: LOOK UP!

1. Pray for insight; then read Colossians 3:1–4:1, which is our focus for the week.

> **3:1** Therefore, if you have been raised with Christ, keep seeking the things above, where Christ is, seated at the right hand of God. **3:2** Keep thinking about things above, not things on the earth, **3:3** for you have died and your life is hidden with Christ in God. **3:4**

When Christ (who is your life) appears, then you too will be revealed in glory with him. **3:5** So put to death whatever in your nature belongs to the earth: sexual immorality, impurity, shameful passion, evil desire, and greed which is idolatry. **3:6** Because of these things the wrath of God is coming on the sons of disobedience. **3:7** You also lived your lives in this way at one time, when you used to live among them. **3:8** But now, put off all such things as anger, rage, malice, slander, abusive language from your mouth. **3:9** Do not lie to one another since you have put off the old man with its practices **3:10** and have been clothed with the new man that is being renewed in knowledge according to the image of the one who created it. **3:11** Here there is neither Greek nor Jew, circumcised or uncircumcised, barbarian, Scythian, slave or free, but Christ is all and in all.

**3:12** Therefore, as the elect of God, holy and dearly loved, clothe yourselves with a heart of mercy, kindness, humility, gentleness, and patience, **3:13** bearing with one another and forgiving one another, if someone happens to have a complaint against anyone else. Just as the Lord has forgiven you, so you also forgive others. **3:14** And to all these virtues add love, which is the perfect bond. **3:15** Let the peace of Christ be in control in your heart (for you were in fact called as one body to this peace), and be thankful. **3:16** Let the word of Christ dwell in you richly, teaching and exhorting one another with all wisdom, singing psalms, hymns, and spiritual songs, all with grace in your hearts to God. **3:17** And whatever you do in word or deed, do it all in the name of the Lord Jesus, giving thanks to God the Father through him.

**3:18** Wives, submit to your husbands, as is fitting in the Lord. **3:19** Husbands, love your wives and do not be embittered against them. **3:20** Children, obey your parents in everything, for this is pleasing in the Lord. **3:21** Fathers, do not provoke your children, so they will not become disheartened. **3:22** Slaves, obey your earthly masters in every respect, not only when they are watching—like those who are strictly people-pleasers—but with a sincere heart, fearing the Lord. **3:23** Whatever you are doing, work at it with enthusiasm, as to the Lord and not for people, **3:24** because you know that you will receive your inheritance from the Lord as the reward. Serve the Lord Christ. **3:25** For the one who does wrong will be repaid for his wrong, and there are no exceptions. **4:1** Masters, treat your slaves with justice and fairness, because you know that you also have a master in heaven.

Paul is about to draw conclusions from what he has been saying. Who is Christ? The fullness of deity, he says. Christ is God. What has

He done? Freed us from the dominion of darkness, made us complete, released both Jew and Gentile from lists of rules to follow before approaching Him. Christ-followers have been buried and resurrected with Him, and that should make a difference in our lives.

1. To what does "Therefore" (3:1) refer? Flip back to last week's verses to discover to what this new section connects.

_____

_____

_____

2. Paul writes, "If you have been raised with Christ . . . " (3:1). What follows is for those who have "died" to themselves and are "raised" in newness of life. They have not yet passed into literal heaven, but spiritually they have entered a new kingdom where their lives are radically different. Have you been raised in Christ? If not, do you want to be? Tell Him so.

_____

_____

- *Seated at the right hand of God.* The phrase is an anthropomorphism. (Say that six-syllable word six times and you might make your lip bleed!) We use anthropomorphisms when we attribute human characteristics to nonhumans. If I say an owl waved its hand or my cat burned its fingers, I'm using anthropomorphisms.

We know God is a Spirit who's everywhere (see John 4:24; Eph. 4:4; Ps. 139:7–10; Eph. 1:23), so it's impossible for Him to have a right hand. Yet the author uses this and other figures of speech, using what we know in our finite way to help us understand a God who is infinite. Today when we hear the expression "He's my right-hand man," we probably envision someone who's the speaker's most useful helper. Yet that's not exactly the image "right hand of God" would have conjured up in the minds of first-century believers. These Christians lived under the rule of an emperor. Sitting at the ruler's right hand was not a position of assisting or helping but of ruling. It was associated with words like authority, honor, power, and the submission of others. Consider these words by Peter: "[Jesus] has gone into heaven and is at the right hand of God, angels and authorities and powers having been made subject to him" (1 Pet. 3:22, NJKV).

In Jesus' earthly state, He emptied Himself and submitted to His earthly parents and earthly rulers; He learned obedience. Yet after His resurrection, He tells His disciples that all authority in heaven and earth has been given to Him (Matt. 28:18). He has been restored to His original position and is seated, which shows his work is done. Being seated at the right hand of God is an exalted position, above all humans and angels and every other created being. The apostle John quotes Jesus: "The one who conquers, I will grant him to sit with me on my throne, as I also conquered and sat down with my Father on his throne" (Rev. 3:21, ESV). Our Lord sits at the right hand of the Father on a throne they share. And Hebrews 4:16 tells us it's a throne that we may approach with confidence to receive mercy and grace to help in time of need. What other king makes an offer like that?

3. In Colossians 3:1–2, what two things does Paul tell his readers they must do? What are they not to do?

Do:

_____

Do:

_____

Don't do:

_____

4. In his book *The Rest of God*, pastor Mark Buchanan describes how Zacchaeus changed his focus after having met Christ. Remember the story? Buchanan writes it this way:

> Zacchaeus was Jericho's runtish tax collector who went out on a limb for Jesus. He shimmied up the trunk of a sycamore tree, scrambled out on its branches, and perched there baboonlike just to catch a glimpse of Jesus. Jesus liked

him, though no one else in town apparently did. Jesus asked him to get down from that tree immediately: "I want to come to your house today."

"Look, Lord!" Zacchaeus says in response. "Here and now I give half of my possessions to the poor, and if I have cheated anybody out of anything, I will pay back four times the amount" (Luke 19:8). Zacchaeus meets Jesus and changes his mind, but straight on the heels of that, he changes his ways. He embraces a practice that embodies and rehearses his new way of seeing. Jesus's comment on the matter is telling: "Today salvation has come to this house" (Luke 19:9). When salvation comes to your house, first you think differently, then you act differently. First you shift the imagination with which you perceive this world, and then you enact gestures with which you honor it."[7]

At Dallas Theological Seminary, I teach a class on the role of women in ministry. One of my single students had been warned all about the dangers of radical feminism, but no one had ever taught her that God made her, as a woman, in His own image! When we covered that part of Genesis in class, she raised her hand and asked a profound question: "You mean I don't have to be married to be fully in God's image?"

"No way."

Her lip quivered. "And I don't have to become a mom before I can be fully complete in Christ?"

"Absolutely not."

She started to weep, the joy in her heart spilling out of her eyes. Not one thing in her external circumstances had changed, but truth had filled her mind, changing her priorities and her view of herself. Now she has a passion to tell other women the life-changing truth of their creation in God's image. She writes blog entries and articles about it and speaks on the subject. When truth entered her mind, she quit making "husband finding" her main goal and instead made ministering to others her main concern.

With what truth do you need to fill your mind? What captures your imagination? (When your mind wanders, where does it go?) List some ways you can fill your mind with the truth.

---

[7] Mark Buchanan, *The Rest of God* (Nashville: W Publishing Group, 2006), 7.

5. In her book *Prayer Is a Place*, Phyllis Tickle says, "What a limited and chipped lens one person's mind is for reflecting the world to itself."[8] What masters we are at deceiving ourselves. That's why we need regular intake of God's truth through the Word and interaction with fellow believers. How much of a priority are these for you? How well do your actions line up with your priorities?

6. What reasons does Paul give for why his readers are to set their minds on and seek "above" things (Col. 3:3, 4, 9–10)?

• *Hidden with Christ in God.* One of the benefits of salvation in Christ is being "hidden" with Him. My obstetrician friend, Dr. Bill Cutrer, explains:

> In the hospital where I used to practice, our neonatal nursery was about thirty yards from the operating suites. Often following stabilization of an extremely premature infant, one of our neonatologists would scoop up the baby in comparatively huge hands and run the hallway to the neonatal intensive care unit. At the close of the case after getting the mother safely to recovery, I'd go to the nursery to check on the infant. The first time I did, I was struck by the image of the tiny, struggling infant as he responded to the physician. As the doctor checked its reflexes by moving his thumb to touch the baby's palm, the tiny hand grasped that finger. Then, almost in reflexive response, the physician's huge mitt

[8] Phyllis Tickle, *Prayer Is a Place: America's Religious Landscape Observed* (New York: Doubleday, 2005), 71.

wrapped around the tiny baby's hand. That touch of compassion reminded me of Jesus' promise that no one could snatch his children out of the Father's hand (John 10:29). Similarly, as we cling to Christ as the baby clings to the thumb, God the Father wraps His hand around us. We are hidden with Christ in God. And it's a paradox . . . while we're hidden in Him, He reveals Himself to others through us.

7. What promise does Paul give in Colossians 3:4? What do you think that will be like?

---

---

## TUESDAY: PUT OFF BUT NOT PUT OUT

1. Pray for insight; then read today's verses.

> **3:5** So put to death whatever in your nature belongs to the earth: sexual immorality, impurity, shameful passion, evil desire, and greed which is idolatry. **3:6** Because of these things the wrath of God is coming on the sons of disobedience. **3:7** You also lived your lives in this way at one time, when you used to live among them. **3:8** But now, put off all such things as anger, rage, malice, slander, abusive language from your mouth. **3:9** Do not lie to one another since you have put off the old man with its practices **3:10** and have been clothed with the new man that is being renewed in knowledge according to the image of the one who created it. **3:11** Here there is neither Greek nor Jew, circumcised or uncircumcised, barbarian, Scythian, slave or free, but Christ is all and in all.

2. Those who have "died" with and "been raised" with Christ and are "hidden" with him (3:1–3) should live changed lives just as Zacchaeus did. As a result of our status with Christ, what are we His followers to put to death (3:5)?

---

---

3. In the Hebrew portion of the Bible, the Old Testament, we see wealth described as having a change of clothing (so people had something to wear when they did laundry) and food for the next meal without having first to earn it. This standard is still true, as most people on the planet live on less than two dollars per day. With this in mind, how wealthy are you? How generous are you with your earthly goods?

_____

_____

_____

4. Paul equates greed with idol worship. An idol can be anything that's more important to us than God. Why do you think Paul makes this greed/idolatry connection? What are some signs that people "worship the almighty dollar"?

_____

_____

_____

5. Consider the list below. Rate how you are doing at "putting to death" these practices. Commit, by God's grace, to turn from these and make restitution, where necessary.

   Sexual immorality
   Impurity
   Shameful passion
   Evil desire
   Greed that takes the form of idolatry

6. What does Paul say will happen to those who commit such acts (3:6)?

_____

_____

7. What tense does Paul use in 3:7? Why do you think he does so?

_____

_____

8. Paul starts with a death/resurrection image and talks about putting some practices to death. Then he changes to a wardrobe metaphor with putting off and putting on. One takes off dirty old clothing and changes into clean new garments. What are believers to take off or put off (Col. 3:8, 9)?

_____

_____

_____

9. Abraham Lincoln said, "When angry, count ten. When very angry, count one hundred." Mark Twain said, "When angry, count ten. When very angry, cuss." Are you more like Lincoln or Twain? How do you handle anger?

_____

_____

10. What reason does Paul give for why Christ-followers should turn away from the sins listed in this passage (3:9)?

_____

_____

11. In what is the believer renewed and according to whom (3:10)?

_____

_____

12. The proto-Gnostics, who had significant influence in Colossae when Paul wrote, believed in higher, secret knowledge that was unavailable to the average person. What does Paul say is the source of knowledge, and what access do believers have to it (3:10)?

_____

_____

_____

13. Remember the verses we considered last week—where Paul insists that Gentile Christians do not have to practice Jewish law to be right with God? The mystery religions focused on externals too. Because of these influences, many in Colossae focused on external practices, such as giving up certain foods (like roast pig) and drink, yet their focus should have been on the inner person. What are some externals that make us think, *That person is really close to God*? (Church attendance? Fasting? Long prayers?)

_____

_____

_____

Pray for God to strengthen your inner person, to refocus your priorities to heavenly pursuits—not to gain favor with God but because you already have gained it through Christ.

14. Clearly Paul expects believers to act differently from unbelievers. Yet he criticizes a mindset that focuses on externals. How do we reconcile the two?

_____

_____

_____

15. We can find lots of ways to direct our minds so we think about heavenly things. We can memorize Scripture, listen to worship music, fellowship with other believers. (Note that these things are a means to an end, not the goal.) List one thing in each category below that can help you set your mind on "things above" (3:1, 2), and then pray for God's strength to do so.

*Imagination.* What kind of music or literature or even books on tape can feed your imagination and help you set your mind on heaven?

_____

_____

_____

*Conversation.* With whom will you have a conversation about spiritual things?

_____

_____

_____

*Friendship.* Name something you'd like to see happen in one of your friendships to make the relationship more Christ focused.

_____

_____

_____

*Work.* How can you be more Christlike in the workplace or working at home? Name one task that you dread which you need to do as unto the Lord.

_____

_____

*Recreation.* What one thing can you do this week to redirect recreational time to make it more "above-focused"?

_____

_____

_____

16. What groupings of people does Paul include as those who are made equal through Christ (3:11)?

_____

_____

_____

The apostle breaks these lists of people into four groups. Three of them contrast with each other: Jew and Greek; circumcised and uncircumcised; slave and free. He also includes barbarian and Scythian, who aren't in contrast with each other but complete the list of people with whom Paul's readers would have had contact.

Up to this point in salvation history, there have been two major people groups: Jew and Greek (or circumcised and uncircumcised). To the Jews, *Greeks* included "barbarians and Scythians" and all were considered Gentiles—a broad category that included all non-Jews. Yet in Colossians, Paul has different categorizations in mind. Here, *Greek* is not the same as *Gentile*, but probably means "non-Jewish person of specifically Greek origin and culture." Then Paul adds the missing Gentiles in the equation—"barbarian and Scythian." He's saying that Jews, cultured Greeks, uncultured Gentiles, slaves, and free people all are equal at the foot of the cross. All in Christ are unified and equal, regardless of race or nationality.

Later Paul tells masters to treat their slaves fairly. No matter what our position, being a Christian changes how we view others. Christians who owned slaves were not to view profits like others did because they weren't to view people as others did. Slaves were not to be viewed as human tools, as Aristotle claimed. They were to be seen as people made in God's image, possessing innate worth and dignity.

A Christian who lives today in Monaco, one of the world's richest countries, has described how yacht owners and yacht workers fellowship joyfully together. What never happens in private yacht clubs—such affectionate intermingling of people in widely diverse social positions—happens freely in the church. As those who serve the same Lord and Master, as those who are children of the same Father, Christ-followers have unique reasons to serve one another humbly, no matter what their race or socioeconomic status.

• *Scythian.* According to the *Theological Dictionary of the New Testament,* Scythians were originally Iranian nomads who invaded Asia Minor about 750 years before Paul wrote. They terrorized those in the Near East without establishing any lasting kingdom. Their alliance with Babylon enabled the latter to overthrow Assyria. By colonizing the north shore of the Black Sea, the Greeks made contact with the Scythians, whom they regarded as a simple and strong people, but also crude, cruel, and uncultured. Later *Scythian* was used to mean slaves from an area located near the Black Sea. Paul's use of *Scythian* here may be borrowed from an ancient baptismal liturgy, which in praise and thanksgiving celebrates the new humanity and its elimination of all distinctions. Whether barbarians and Scythians are distinguished or the Scythians are an outstanding example of barbarians is debatable.[9] In any case, their baptism into Christ made them equal.

17. How do you think the leveling of all these groups as equal was supposed to affect their attitudes and interactions?

_____

_____

18. Why do you think it would be wrong, then and now, to treat others for whom Christ died as second-class citizens based on nationality or race?

_____

_____

[9] G. Kittel, G. Friedrich, and G. W. Bromiley, translators; *Theological Dictionary of the New Testament* (Grand Rapids: W. B. Eerdmans, 1985, 1995).

Does your life line up with God's view of racism? What are some ways you can help put an end to racism?

_____

_____

_____

## WEDNESDAY: PUT ONS

1. Pray for insight; then read today's verses.

> **Colossians 3:12** Therefore, as the elect of God, holy and dearly loved, clothe yourselves with a heart of mercy, kindness, humility, gentleness, and patience, **3:13** bearing with one another and forgiving one another, if someone happens to have a complaint against anyone else. Just as the Lord has forgiven you, so you also forgive others. **3:14** And to all these virtues add love, which is the perfect bond. **3:15** Let the peace of Christ be in control in your heart (for you were in fact called as one body to this peace), and be thankful. **3:16** Let the word of Christ dwell in you richly, teaching and exhorting one another with all wisdom, singing psalms, hymns, and spiritual songs, all with grace in your hearts to God. **3:17** And whatever you do in word or deed, do it all in the name of the Lord Jesus, giving thanks to God the Father through him.

2. Circle where Paul uses these words or forms of them: *peace*, *forgive*, and *thank*. Why do you think he emphasizes these when speaking of unity in Christ?

_____

_____

_____

_____

_____

3. Why does Paul include the word "therefore" (3:12)? That is, on the basis of what truth does he tell his readers to put on beautiful characteristics?

_____

_____

_____

4. What three words does Paul use in verse 12 to describe believers?

_____

_____

*Elect.* To be called elect is quite an honor. Sometimes it's misunderstood to mean "exclusively superior," yet it has quite the opposite sense. Lest one brag or feel smug about how brilliant he or she was to "choose" God or "accept Christ" (as if the Lord passed muster), the apostle comes along and says that those who call on Christ for salvation (from our point of view) were actually chosen (from God's point of view) for divine mercy or favor. We responded to an irresistible call. That should make us thankful. Often we ask, Why me? when trials come. Being elect should make us ask, Why me? for God's unexplainable kindness to us.

5. Previously we considered what behaviors a believer should "put off"—habits such as anger and immorality. Now we consider what to "put on" in light of our new identity as the elect, the holy, the loved. In what does Paul say a believer must be dressed (v. 12)?

_____

_____

It's been said that charity is tax deductible, but mercy is time consuming. Describe a time when someone demonstrated mercy or compassion to you. What opportunities do you have to show mercy?

_____

_____

_____

To be kind is to have a gracious attitude with moral uprightness. Whom do you know who's kind? How does he or she demonstrate kindness? To whom can you be kind?

_____

_____

_____

_____

Humility is a willingness to become low. A quick survey of Israel's history demonstrates time and again how humble people (think shepherd-boy David) win against the proud people (think giant Goliath). God hates pride, actively opposing it, yet He gives grace to the humble. In what areas do you struggle with pride or false pride? How do you respond when people treat you like you're low?

_____

_____

_____

_Gentle_ is not a synonym for _weak_. It's to be kindly and moderate and is the opposite of severe or violent. What triggers harshness in you? Are you gentle in how you speak? In how you touch? In your tone of voice? To whom can you purposefully show gentleness?

_____

_____

_____

What makes you impatient in traffic? With family members? In a restaurant? When on the phone? At other times?

_____

_____

_____

Describe the most patient person you know.

_____

_____

_____

Picture yourself physically putting on these qualities: mercy, kindness, humility, gentleness, patience, love. Consider putting this list by your mirror or in your closet to remind you as you dress to put on the apparel God considers essential.

6. What two descriptions of Christ-followers does Paul add in 3:13?

_____

_____

_____

7. Paul tells the Colossian believers they should be "bearing with one another." To bear is to endure or hold up. Whose burden can you help to endure? How?

_____

_____

_____

8. Paul also says we should be "forgiving one another." I found it difficult to forgive the woman whose kids spray-painted my car. (She promised to pay for it, insisting she was a "good Christian." Then she promptly moved without leaving a forwarding address.) Forgiveness sounds great until we have to actually do it! Against whom do you have a complaint? Release your complaint to God, asking Him to bless those who have injured you.

_____

_____

9. How does Paul say we are to forgive (3:13)? Why do you think it's so important to do so?

_____

_____

_____

10. What is the great virtue that Christians are to add to all others, and how is it described (3:14)? Why do you think Paul gives it this description?

_____

_____

_____

11. The apostle tells his readers to let something control their hearts, in addition to putting on a new wardrobe. He seems to have more than just something internal in mind.

What is that something (3:15)?

_____

_____

What is its connection to interpersonal oneness (3:15)?

_____

_____

_____

Sometimes we think of a calling as relating only to occupational ministry. Yet Paul says all believers are called to something. What is that calling (3:15)?

_____

What hinders you from having peace in your heart? In your relationships?

_____

_____

_____

12. To dwell is to make a permanent home. What is the imperative in Colossians 3:16, and how is it to be demonstrated?

_____

_____

_____

13. Memory verses are included in this study to help you obey this command to have the "word of Christ" dwelling in you richly. Take some time to review your verse for this week and last.

14. Christ-followers are to teach and exhort one another in all wisdom as demonstrations of the "word of Christ" making its permanent home in us. Share a time when someone taught you a life-changing truth from God's Word. With whom can you share Scripture from your heart?

_____

_____

_____

15. As an outgrowth of the Word richly dwelling in believers, we are to sing—not necessarily because we have beautiful voices but because worship is a lovely sacrifice to God. What three kinds of music does Paul list that are to be part of worship (3:16)?

_____

_____

How and to whom do believers sing?

_____

_____

_____

What is loaded in your MP3 or CD player or cassette? How can you use technology to get the Word of God into your heart through "psalms, hymns, and spiritual songs"?

_____

_____

_____

16. Finally, Paul sums up his description of the behavior that should characterize a Christian. What does it look like for all one's deeds to be done in the name of the Lord Jesus? How do your actions measure up?

_____

To whom and through whom are Christians to give thanks (v. 17)?

_____

_____

_____

17. At the end of 3:15, Paul tells the Colossians to be thankful. He repeats the idea in 3:16 (have gratitude) and 3:17 (give thanks)—three verses in a row. Thankfulness is the antidote to discontentment. For what are you thankful? Spend some time really thinking about it. Pray and tell the Father through the Son what you appreciate. What person can you tell, "I'm thankful for you because . . . "?

_____

_____

_____

## THURSDAY: ALL IN THE FAMILY

1. Pray for insight; then read today's verses.

> **Colossians 3:18** Wives, submit to your husbands, as is fitting in the Lord. **3:19** Husbands, love your wives and do not be embittered against them. **3:20** Children, obey your parents in everything, for this is pleasing in the Lord. **3:21** Fathers, do not provoke your children, so they will not become disheartened. **3:22** Slaves, obey your earthly masters in every respect, not only when they are watching—like those who are strictly people-pleasers—but with a sincere heart, fearing the Lord. **3:23** Whatever you are doing, work at it with enthusiasm, as to the Lord and not for people, **3:24** because you know that you will receive your inheritance from the Lord as the reward. Serve the Lord Christ. **3:25** For the one who does wrong will be repaid for his wrong, and there are no exceptions. **4:1** Masters, treat your slaves with justice and fairness, because you know that you also have a master in heaven.

2. Circle all the nouns that identify groups of family members.

3. Did you include slaves and masters? If not, do. Some wonder why Paul would include employee/boss relationships in a section on family life. But keep in mind that the letter to the Colossians was also going with the letter to Philemon. The church apparently met in his home. So when Paul wrote to the Colossians, he had in mind the household structure of Philemon's family, in which slaves and masters lived under the same roof as was the custom in households of the elite.

In his award-winning article "The Cultural Context for Ephesians 5:18–6:9," biblical scholar Gordon Fee gives some background:

> What is important for our purposes is [the book of Ephesians'] clear association with Colossians and, therefore, with Philemon. One of the unfortunate things that happened in the organizing of the Christian canon was the separation of Philemon from Colossians, for both letters would have been read together in Philemon's house church, with both Philemon [master] and Onesimus [slave] present. The point, of course, is that the so-called house rules that occur only in Colossians and Ephesians almost certainly spring from the circumstances that brought Onesimus back to Philemon's household and thus back to his house church.[10]

The house rules Fee has in mind are the family instructions that make up today's reading.

In his writing, Paul has just described Christian worship. Remember? We had the word of Christ dwelling richly and the readers instructing each other, singing psalms, hymns, and spiritual songs. With that as the backdrop, Paul turns to consider relationships in the household. In doing so, he closely links Christian worship with family relationships.

Through Paul's instructions, we see family life taking on a new level of unity. Keep in mind that the culture to which he writes is not inspired, but God's words are. And notice that Paul chooses to address several times the family member with the most societal power—the husband/father/master. As master under Roman law, the householder had absolute rule in the sense that no one else under his roof had any

---

[10] Gordon Fee, "The Cultural Context for Ephesians 5:18–6:9," *Priscilla Papers* Winter 2002 (16:1), 3.

legal means through which to address grievances. The home was not a place of refuge or consumption but the center of economic activity, of production. At marriage the average man was thirty; the average woman, eighteen. Marriage did not happen because of romance but as a means of producing legitimate heirs. Most men—and often their wives—were promiscuous. Wives did not dine with their husbands but ate in separate spaces. Slaves, the spoils of war, homeschooled the legitimate children. The householder, as we shall call him, determined whom the family (including slaves) would worship.

In each pairing of instructions to those living in such a set up, Paul addresses every family member, but each time he comes back to the householder and tells him what it looks like to follow Christ in each of his relationships with those in a vulnerable position.

With this in mind, it's easier to see how Paul's words would have been perceived as radical at the time they were received. Paul does not condone slavery or a world in which women have no legal rights and children are "seen but not heard," but he does assume his readers will be good testimonies within the established social order that includes all three circumstances. Within that order, he gives some expected instructions to the vulnerable: they are to cooperate with a good attitude. Then he gives some shocking instructions to the powerful: they are to treat the vulnerable members of their families kindly, and in marriage the powerful one is even called to lay down his life! (Remember, *agape* is self-sacrificing love.) Within that context, then, we take a closer look at Paul's words.

3. What is the command to wives (3:18) and what are the two commands to husbands (3:19)?

**Wives**                                    **Husbands**

---

---

Paul says a wife's submission is fitting in the Lord (3:18). The word for *fitting* could also be translated as *proper* or *seemly*. Paul uses it in Philemon 1:8 when he expresses confidence that Philemon will do what is proper with his now-returned runaway slave, Onesimus. Here the apostle may mean that in cases where submission would be unseemly, wives should not submit; they should submit only in those ways that are proper in the Lord. Consider Sapphira, who helped her husband lie to the Holy Spirit and was killed for her submission (see Acts 5:8–10). Another possibility, however, is that Paul is simply saying that submission itself is fitting, Christlike behavior for a householder's wife.

Notice Paul uses *obey* with children and slaves, but he chooses a different word for wives. As discussed earlier, to submit is not the same as thing as to obey, although at times it may look the same.

4. What commands does Paul give to children and fathers (3:20–21)?

**Children**                                    **Fathers**

_____

_____

5. What reasons are given for the children's and fathers' commands (3:20–21)?

**Children**                                    **Fathers**

_____

_____

- *Provoke.* This word has also been translated *exasperate.*

6. Notice Paul does not qualify the children's obedience (3:20). Yet what level of spiritual maturity does he assume about the parents whose children he commands to obey (3:14–17)?

_____

_____

_____

Today parents may drop off their children at church and return home to take a nap, or they may send their children to a youth group at a different church from the one they themselves attend. That wouldn't have happened in first-century Colossae. Paul assumes children are worshiping with their parents, as the families—including slaves—followed whatever religion the householder chose.

7. What commands and reasons for such commands are given to slaves and masters (3:22–4:1)?

| Slaves | Masters |
| --- | --- |
|  |  |
|  |  |
|  |  |

• *Justice.* Justice in the legal sense is not quite the idea here (4:1); the thought is *righteous.* According to Paul, masters needed to do more than Roman law required. Rather than going by industry standards, masters were to do what was right, equitable, appropriate, knowing they, too, had a master to whom they would have to give account.

Jewish slavery was different from Roman slavery in that the Jews had no jails, so an indebted person became the lender's slave. According to the Law, Jews had to set their slaves free every seven years. The Greeks had no such system; they took people slaves when they conquered other nations. Their mindset was that slaves were owned tools, not fellow humans created in God's image. Roman slaves didn't get inheritances, which is why Paul emphasized their heavenly inheritance from Christ (Col. 3:24).

Many have asked why Paul didn't tell slaves in the Roman Empire to revolt. To overturn the system would have been a social impossibility—on par with telling Christians in Iraq under Saddam Hussein to overthrow their government rather than live with oppression. It would have been suicide. In Paul's first letter to the Corinthians, he told slaves not to worry about their slavery but to pursue their freedom if they had a chance to be free (1 Cor. 7:21). Rather than overthrowing structures, Paul advised Christians to live within the established governmental order and to effect changes through the gospel and justice systems, not through violence or rebellion.

While we see clearly established levels of rank and authority in the household, social, racial, and economic barriers were and are irrelevant in the church. Slaves and masters worshiped together on Sunday and assumed their household roles on Monday.

At this point, it's good to stop and consider how we read instructions given in a culture that differs so much from the twenty-first-century West. We need some direction in applying the truth of the gospel in our own situations.

Our study of the Bible requires three steps. First we do exegesis—seeking to explain what an author meant when he wrote and how the audience would have understood his words. Next we do what's called the theological step. That is, we determine what part of God's character is behind practices that apply to all believers for all time. We often leave out this step, but we should not. For example, if Paul tells the Colossians to be thankful, we know a thankful attitude is still necessary two thousand years later. But if Paul tells masters to be kind, we don't assume we should go out and buy some humans to try to model our households after those of the Colossians Christians; we try to figure out what in the text is cultural and what is transferable to our time based on the character of God. What is timeless and what's time bound? Finally, we apply the timeless truth to our own situation once we know what's transferable.

Let's walk through this process considering the slavery question. Paul tells slaves to obey. It's safe to say that in all places where Christians are owned, they should obey rather than, say, murder or steal from or even cop attitudes with their masters. We should not conclude that because slaves were to obey, a modern-day application is "Employees, obey your employers." Employees generally do not live with their employers. And whereas a slave is prohibited from walking off the job, usually an employee may legally do so. That gives employees a status of equality where their submission is voluntary. Not so with slaves, who rank under their masters and must obey. So while we can draw some principles about how to act when in a position of lesser social power, we must be clear about what the differences are.

If we go straight from interpreting imperatives for those in different times to applying these imperatives in modern-day settings, we risk misapplication, such as "Paul told slaves to obey their masters, so we need to obey our employers." What we *can* conclude is this: From those in positions of greater societal power, Paul expects humility, gentleness, and even self-sacrifice because God Himself is humble, gentle, and self-sacrificing. From those in positions of lesser social power, Paul expects attitudes of cooperation and confidence that demonstrate a belief that God is just.

## FRIDAY: PAUL TO PHILEMON

1. Pray for insight; then read Paul's letter to Philemon. Remember that it was sent to the owner of a runaway slave in Colossae, along with the epistle to the Colossians.

**Philemon 1:1** From Paul, a prisoner of Christ Jesus, and Timothy our brother, to Philemon, our dear friend and colaborer, **1:2** to Apphia our sister, to Archippus our fellow soldier, and to the church that meets in your house. **1:3** Grace and peace to you from God our Father and the Lord Jesus Christ!

**1:4** I always thank my God as I remember you in my prayers, **1:5** because I hear of your faith in the Lord Jesus and your love for all the saints. **1:6** I pray that the faith you share with us may deepen your understanding of every blessing that belongs to you in Christ. **1:7** I have had great joy and encouragement because of your love, for the hearts of the saints have been refreshed through you, brother.

**1:8** So, although I have quite a lot of confidence in Christ and could command you to do what is proper, **1:9** I would rather appeal to you on the basis of love—I, Paul, an old man and even now a prisoner for the sake of Christ Jesus—**1:10** I am appealing to you concerning my child, whose spiritual father I have become during my imprisonment, that is, Onesimus, **1:11** who was formerly useless to you, but is now useful to you and me. **1:12** I have sent him (who is my very heart) back to you. **1:13** I wanted to keep him so that he could serve me in your place during my imprisonment for the sake of the gospel. **1:14** However, without your consent I did not want to do anything, so that your good deed would not be out of compulsion, but from your own willingness. **1:15** For perhaps it was for this reason that he was separated from you for a little while, so that you would have him back eternally, **1:16** no longer as a slave, but more than a slave, as a dear brother. He is especially so to me, and even more so to you now, both humanly speaking and in the Lord. **1:17** Therefore if you regard me as a partner, accept him as you would me. **1:18** Now if he has defrauded you of anything or owes you anything, charge what he owes to me. **1:19** I, Paul, have written this letter with my own hand: I will repay it. I could also mention that you owe me your very self. **1:20** Yes, brother, let me have some benefit from you in the Lord. Refresh my heart in Christ. **1:21** Since I was confident that you would obey, I wrote to you, because I knew that you would do even more than what I am asking you to do. **1:22** At the same time also, prepare a place for me to stay, for I hope that through your prayers I will be given back to you.

**1:23** Epaphras, my fellow prisoner in Christ Jesus, greets you. **1:24** Mark, Aristarchus, Demas and Luke, my colaborers, greet you too. **1:25** May the grace of the Lord Jesus Christ be with your spirit.

2. Now read this background material.

Paul's epistle to Philemon, which we refer to as the book of Philemon, has a total of only twenty-five verses. The author refers to himself as Paul three times (in verses 1, 9 and 19). So we know the apostle wrote it—probably in AD 60. This was most likely during his first imprisonment in Rome.

As an exercise in one of my writing classes, I ask my students to imagine what it would be like to stand in Philemon's shoes. His slave runs away; then later Philemon opens the door to find him standing there. As if that weren't enough of a surprise, Philemon then hears that Onesimus made it all the way to Rome, where he met up with Paul, who shared the gospel with him. So Onesimus risked death to return and obey his master. I ask my students to get in groups and imagine Philemon's response. What would a letter back to Paul be like? Here are some examples of what they come up with:

*Assuming Philemon chose not to forgive*

Philemon, an overworked, underpaid, recently dispossessed servant-leader. To Paul, the prisoner who sets captives free.

I wish I could thank you for looking after my asset, Onesimus, but I am displeased with his present condition. He left Colossae as low mileage. After a round trip to Rome, he requires an overhaul. Of course, the return was easier because he lacked the weight of my possessions.

I am very sorry about your bond program. Paul, your stock may have increased, but mine has decreased. Why did you receive multiple dividends when my stock split? One can hardly find good help these days.

Accommodations may not be as posh as you had hoped. Sorry, the Le Meridien folded. Someone freed all the slaves. Since I have to receive Onesimus as a brother, he now has your guest room. I owe you and I will do more than you ask. I will refresh your heart by providing you a posh room with a view—through ornate ironwork.

Your menial worker in Christ, Philemon

### From Philemon "the backslider"

Philemon, a co-prisoner of my brother Paul—servant of our Lord Jesus Christ and gracious apostle to the saints. Greetings from surroundings familiar to you.

You may have questions about current conditions. Forgiveness, please, for the slow reply, but Rome has had my attention for some time. Onesimus arrived, having come upon me in a hovel on the backside of the east end. I have to confess I have been stripped of all possessions. My assets have been confiscated, and our brother Onesimus was among them. You see, my gambling consumed me and Rome caught up. The establishments in Colossae are not quite as comfortable as those there. I've heard a rumor about a transfer. Perhaps we will see one another sooner than you hoped. As for Onesimus, I've heard he's been purchased by the governor. I'm sure he is serving wine and flatbread as I write.

The grace of the Lord Jesus Christ be with your Spirit.

### Assuming better of Philemon

I, Philemon, along with the church that meets in my house, greet you, Paul, a prisoner of the Lord Jesus Christ. Grace and peace to you from God the Father. Onesimus arrived smelling clean as ocean air with your letter, and the news filled my household and me with unspeakable joy. We cooked the fatted lamb and seasoned it with wine. We praise God for Onesimus' return and for his newfound freedom in Jesus Christ our Lord.

Once again, Paul, you bless me—not only are we overjoyed that you led Onesimus to Christ; we thank God for your guidance in returning him to us. With respect to his indebtedness, we require nothing. All is forgiven. We celebrate our new brother in Christ. We have released him from his bond-service that he might fully serve our Lord. The church at my house embraces him as a brother. We commit to help him grow in the grace and knowledge of our Lord Jesus Christ.

Your room is prepared and ready. May God grant your release so that we may rejoice together! I, Philemon, write this with my own hand.

PS. Could you send the towels he took to Rome so he can return them to the Hilton Colossae?

3. Imagine what this story would have been like from the point of view of Onesimus, the slave who runs away, travels to faraway Rome, meets up with Paul, comes to Christ, and must return to face possible death. On your own notebook paper, write out your understanding of what that might have been like and the different possible outcomes. If you like to write, consider crafting a letter similar to those above.

## SATURDAY: HARD AT WORK VS. HARDLY WORKING

**Scripture:** "Slaves, obey your earthly masters in every respect, not only when they are watching—like those who are strictly people-pleasers—but with a sincere heart, fearing the Lord. Whatever you are doing, work at it with enthusiasm, as to the Lord and not for people, because you know that you will receive your inheritance from the Lord as the reward. Serve the Lord Christ. For the one who does wrong will be repaid for his wrong, and there are no exceptions." (Col. 3:22–25)

"Slaves, obey your earthly masters." On the one hand, we shouldn't teach this as Paul's direct command to employees, as we've said. On the other hand, much in Paul's advice applies to today's workers, who spend more than 46 percent of their waking hours on the job. While social structures that allowed slavery are history in the West, this advice endures: "Whatever you are doing, work at it with enthusiasm, as to the Lord and not for people."

Paul's advice includes a warning about toiling only when the master is watching. Reading it reminds me of a time when I worked for a financial services corporation to put my husband through graduate school. One day my boss's boss called him to say, "Look busy. The senior vice president is heading to your floor." That call frustrated my boss, a Christian, who asked no one in particular, "What? Does he think I drop my pants whenever the senior vice president isn't here?"

Is slavery timeless? No. Is working hard even when nobody's watching a timeless value? Absolutely.

I toured the Washington National Cathedral as a young girl, and something our guide pointed out made a lasting impression. She had us arch around to see the back of a statue's head. Even though it was out of view, the hair on the back of that statue was as beautifully crafted as the face. Our guide explained why the sculptor took such care with something he expected no human to notice: "God sees it."

That sculptor did his work "as to the Lord, and not for people."

Eye service isn't always motivated by laziness. Sometimes there's peer pressure. When I worked in human resources, a woman I interviewed told me that in a previous job, she and others who performed well were criticized by co-workers because good performers made the others have to work harder. Many wanted to work only when the supervisors were watching. Serving Christ as master means working hard even when forces from within and without war against us.

If Christ were your boss or supervisor, would your labor look different?

In Scripture we find that work has God-given dignity. Both men and women were tasked with subduing the earth. Work is God's plan for humans, having been instituted before the fall. Sometimes we think work is a result of the fall, but toil is the part that came after sin entered the world.

We rarely hear "how God called me to be an accountant," yet He leads just as directly in so-called secular work as in vocational ministry. I once heard country singer Ricky Skaggs during a concert ask the audience to pray that God would use his music to open doors for the gospel. Martin Luther said, "God milks the cow through you." Another reformer, Zwingli, said, "There's nothing so like God as the worker." Jesus Himself spent much of His earthly life thinking about the marketplace. A carpenter by trade, He met suppliers and provided a product.

In his epistle to Titus, Paul gives a reason for slaves to work hard in addition to the fact that Christians have a heavenly master: to "adorn the doctrine of God" (Titus 2:9–10, NKJV). The way people work can make the gospel attractive. Even though we aren't commanded to obey employers, we need to be good testimonies. So we are to work diligently, even when nobody is watching, and we're to work with enthusiasm and integrity, knowing we have a heavenly master who does require our obedience.

Picture an honest mechanic, a fair news reporter, a trustworthy used car salesman, a just lawyer, a righteous IRS agent, a homemaker who doesn't eat bonbons or lie around watching soaps. The stereotypes exist because it's so rare to find honest, just workers. The good ones stand out as different. I once had to inform a woman she was turned down for promotion because she had a big chip on her shoulder. She defended herself by saying everybody else in her department had a crummy attitude too. She couldn't understand that anybody can have a bad attitude; it's the person with the good attitude who stands out.

Often we pray asking to know God's will about where to work while we ignore what He has clearly revealed about His will—*how* we work. Doing our work well is God's will for us. Monday morning is as important to God as Sunday.

**Prayer:** *Gracious heavenly Father, thank You for being a kind Master. Thank You for being a loving Lord. Thank You that Your Son invites us to boldly approach Your throne that we might receive mercy and grace to help in time of need. Help us to treat others with mercy and equity. Help us never to be bigoted or ungracious or arrogant, knowing You created all humans in Your image. Help us to put off the old person and put on the new, having renewed minds saturated in Your Word. Help us to accurately handle that Word, to take it into our hearts, to live it well. In Your mercy, forgive us where we have failed. Help us to honor You in our family relationships. We ask You to bless the work of our hands. Help us to approach work in a way that honors You, knowing we must give account for what we do. Help us be committed to excellence that we might shine forth Your glory to a broken world in need of Your touch. We ask these things, our Father, in the name of Your Son. Amen.*

**For Memorization:** "Let the word of Christ dwell in you richly, teaching and exhorting one another with all wisdom, singing psalms, hymns, and spiritual songs, all with grace in your hearts to God. And whatever you do in word or deed, do it all in the name of the Lord Jesus, giving thanks to God the Father through him." (Col. 3:16–17)

# WEEK 4 OF 4

*Christ the Door-Opener: Colossians 4:2–18*

## SUNDAY: PRAYER MATTERS

**Scripture:** "Be devoted to prayer, keeping alert in it with thanksgiving." (Col. 4:2)

Back in the late 1990s when my daughter still rode around in a car seat, we had a couple of statewide droughts in Texas that produced widespread crop failure and forced hundreds of cities to implement water rationing. The second time around, more than sixty days passed without one drop from the sky. One afternoon during that time, as I drove us home from the club where I swim, we spotted a grass fire in the median. I pulled out my cell phone and called the fire department pronto.

Several days later, we passed the same stretch of grass, black from the scorch of the blaze. My little girl wanted to know all about it: Should we be scared? Is it bad to call 911? What causes fires? Will it happen again? Why did the grass burn? Why? Why? Why?

I explained that the grass needed a drink—that all the Texas grass needed a drink, that the plants were thirsty, that the trees craved rain.

"What can we do?" she asked.

"All we can do is pray."

"Right now?"

"I suppose," I said. "Now's as good a time as any."

She insisted I pray.

"OK," I said. So I kept my eyes on the road and started talking to God. I told Him about how the grass needed a drink. I reminded Him that the trees were thirsty. And I told Him we were scared we'd run out of water. "Please, God," I pleaded, "We need rain." When I finished, she prayed too, with that childlike, simple faith Jesus commends.

About twenty seconds after we finished, a huge drop splashed on my windshield. I looked around to see if a truck was leaking fluid. Then another drop hit. And another.

Ohmyword! It dawned on me.

"HE SAID YES!" my daughter screamed from the back seat. "HE SAID YES!"

Sure enough, that liquid was coming from the sky, and it was rain. I dabbed my eyes and kept on driving. Others pulled over, got out of their cars, and threw their arms in the air in fits of unbridled joy.

"HE SAID YES!" my daughter kept screaming.

"Yes, He did," I whispered, shaking my head as I marveled at the timing. It seemed so coincidental. (William Temple, the ninety-eighth archbishop of Canterbury, was known to have said, "When I pray, coincidences happen; and when I don't pray, they don't happen.")

James reminded his readers that God hears the prayers of ordinary people: "Elijah was a human being like us, and he prayed earnestly that it would not rain and there was no rain on the land for three years and six months" (James 5:17). Sometimes we get the idea that God answers the prayers of the superspiritual while He glosses over the requests of us lesser mortals. Why should God answer some mom and her little girl driving by a burned median in Texas? Yet that's James's point—Elijah was just like us, and see what his prayers accomplished? Prayer is access to supreme power. If we really grasped that truth, people would have to pry us out of our prayer closets.

In Colossians 4:2, Paul packs a lot of instruction on prayer into one short verse. He says it's something we should be devoted to, alert in, and something we should give thanks with.

To be devoted to something is to persist at it. Paul's word for *devoted to* was used of a boat docked and continually ready for use. To be devoted to prayer is to cling to it with persistent attention and perseverance. That kind of prayer is not the stuff we tack on after the fact when we've run out of all other options. "All we can do is pray," I had said, as if praying is barely a cut above nothing. In *Pilgrim at Tinker Creek*, Annie Dillard writes, "On the whole, I do not find Christians, outside of the catacombs, sufficiently sensible of conditions. Does anyone have the foggiest idea what sort of power we so blithely invoke? Or, as I suspect, does no one believe a word of it? The churches are children playing on the floor with their chemistry sets, making up a batch of TNT to kill a Sunday morning. It is madness to wear straw hats and velvet hats to church; we should all be wearing crash helmets. Ushers should issue life preservers and signal flares; they should lash us to our pews."

Dillard is right. Praying is like lighting dynamite.

If we truly believed that, Paul wouldn't have to remind us to be alert. How many times do we, like the disciples in Gethsemane, doze off during our prayers rather than staying vigilant? I don't know about you, but I doubt I'd doze off near a bomb squad working to dismantle wires before the clock reaches a big red ZERO.

Paul concludes with words about thankfulness. Without gratitude, prayer can degenerate to a "gimme" list: Gimme food; gimme health; gimme a good job. Gimme a good time.

When we speak only of what we want without reflecting on what we've already received, we risk thinking of God as the big Santa Claus in the sky—or worse, a grand cosmic vending machine. We put in our dollar of obedience and expect the car to work, the chicken pox to strike someone else's child, the checkbook to balance. And we throw a tantrum when we pay and bad stuff happens. Thankfulness reminds us that we've already received infinitely more than we put in.

I don't like it when I give and give to my daughter and she forgets to say thank you. Yet so often I take and take from my heavenly Father without a word of appreciation.

For what do you need to pray devotedly, alertly, with thanksgiving? My list is pretty long. What about yours? Why not start now?

## MONDAY: PRAYER IS THE WORK

1. Read the section of Scripture that will be our focus for the week.

> **Colossians 4:2** Be devoted to prayer, keeping alert in it with thanksgiving. **4:3** At the same time pray for us too, that God may

open a door for the message so that we may proclaim the mystery of Christ, for which I am in chains. **4:4** Pray that I may make it known as I should. **4:5** Conduct yourselves with wisdom toward outsiders, making the most of the opportunities. **4:6** Let your speech always be gracious, seasoned with salt, so that you may know how you should answer everyone.

**4:7** Tychicus, a dear brother, faithful minister, and fellow slave in the Lord, will tell you all the news about me. **4:8** I sent him to you for this very purpose, that you may know how we are doing and that he may encourage your hearts. **4:9** I sent him with Onesimus, the faithful and dear brother, who is one of you. They will tell you about everything here.

**4:10** Aristarchus, my fellow prisoner, sends you greetings, as does Mark, the cousin of Barnabas (about whom you received instructions; if he comes to you, welcome him). **4:11** And Jesus who is called Justus also sends greetings. In terms of Jewish converts, these are the only fellow workers for the kingdom of God, and they have been a comfort to me. **4:12** Epaphras, who is one of you and a slave of Christ, greets you. He is always struggling in prayer on your behalf, so that you may stand mature and fully assured in all the will of God. **4:13** For I can testify that he has worked hard for you and for those in Laodicea and Hierapolis. **4:14** Our dear friend Luke the physician and Demas greet you. **4:15** Give my greetings to the brothers and sisters who are in Laodicea and to Nympha and the church that meets in her house. **4:16** And after you have read this letter, have it read to the church of Laodicea. In turn, read the letter from Laodicea as well. **4:17** And tell Archippus, "See to it that you complete the ministry you received in the Lord." **4:18** I, Paul, write this greeting by my own hand. Remember my chains. Grace be with you.

2. What stands out to you in this section of Scripture?

_____

_____

3. What timeless imperatives do you find in 4:2, 5–6?

_____

_____

4. What word does Paul keep emphasizing (Col 3:15–17; 4:2)? Why do you think he does so?

_____

_____

_____

5. Set aside the rest of the time you would normally spend in Bible study today and use it to devote yourself to prayer. Pray alertly with thanksgiving. Be sure to include in your prayers the spread of the good news of God's love through Jesus Christ and those who labor to share it.

## TUESDAY: MORE IMPORTANT THAN FREEDOM

1. Pray for insight; then read the section of Scripture that will be our focus for the day.

> **Colossians 4:3** At the same time pray for us too, that God may open a door for the message so that we may proclaim the mystery of Christ, for which I am in chains. **4:4** Pray that I may make it known as I should. **4:5** Conduct yourselves with wisdom toward outsiders, making the most of the opportunities. **4:6** Let your speech always be gracious, seasoned with salt, so that you may know how you should answer everyone.

2. For what does Paul ask prayer (4:3–4)? Why is this significant in light of the fact that he's jailed and far from home? (If you were in jail far from home, what doors do you think you'd want opened?)

_____

_____

3. Paul previously mentioned the mystery of Christ. Do you remember from Week 2 what the mystery was that he is making known (1:26–27; 2:2–3; 4:3)?

_____

_____

_____

4. Bearing in mind the teaching of mystery religions that abounded in Colossae, why do you think Paul keeps emphasizing the "mystery"?

*Only 0.1 percent of people come to Christ through mass evangelism. Most by far hear about Christ and believe through the witness of someone who talks with them personally.*

_____

_____

5. Even though Paul is imprisoned for spreading the gospel, what is his top priority (4:3–4)?

_____

_____

_____

6. Who do you know or know about who's preaching the gospel and jailed for doing so? Pray for them that God might open doors for the gospel message to spread.

7. How does Paul say believers are to conduct themselves with "outsiders," those outside the faith (4:5)?

_____

_____

_____

- *Making the most of the opportunity.* Other translators have rendered this phrase *redeeming the time.* (T. S. Eliot borrows the phrase for the fourth section of his "Ash Wednesday" conversion poem.) Paul says the same thing in Ephesians 5:16, telling readers to redeem the time "because the days are evil." *Redeeming the time* is a commercial term. It means "to buy up, to ransom, to rescue from loss." The word for *time* is rendered *opportunity* by the NET Bible translators, because that's the idea it carries. It's not chronological time as we think of watching a clock (*chronos*). Rather, it's time in which something is seasonable. It has the idea of taking advantage of a chance that can't be recalled once it's lost. In this context it has to do with having wisdom to see and act on windows of opportunity with unbelievers.

8. How can we make the most of the opportunities to share Christ?

_____

_____

_____

_____

9. What should characterize the believer's speech, according to Paul (4:6)?

_____

_____

_____

• *Seasoned with salt.* Paul uses a metaphor for speech that we should not confuse with the "salty" language that characterizes sailors. Rather, Paul has in mind winsome, witty speech full of moral quality. It's not boring, and not obscene, but humorous and pleasant and intriguing and good. One ancient writer describes academics as having such speech. Today we use rosemary and cloves and peppercorns without much fuss, but people in Paul's day couldn't go to the supermarket and choose from seventy-five spices from several producers; salt was essential to good eating. Imagine unseasoned French fries and crackers and chips. Our speech should be the salt that makes it tough to eat just one.

10. Think of a time when someone spoke to you ungraciously. How did you feel?

_____

_____

_____

11. Share a time when someone spoke gracious, winsome words to you. What effect did those words have on you?

_____

_____

_____

12. What reason does Paul give for having "salty" speech (4:6)?

_____

_____

_____

13. In an era of TVs, DVDs, CDs, and MP3 players with earphones, it's easy to lose the art of conversation. What can you do to gain confidence in your ability to speak winsome words? With whom can you share such words?

_____

_____

_____

14. Pray about your lost friends and how you communicate with them (and not just how you share about Christ with them). Are you winsome in your conversation? Do you talk about edifying topics? Are you

interesting? Ask God to open doors of opportunity and to give you the courage to walk through them.

_____

_____

_____

## WEDNESDAY: THE CAST AND CREW

1. Pray for insight; then read the section of Scripture that will be our focus for the day.

> **Colossians 4:7** Tychicus, a dear brother, faithful minister, and fellow slave in the Lord, will tell you all the news about me. **4:8** I sent him to you for this very purpose, that you may know how we are doing and that he may encourage your hearts. **4:9** I sent him with Onesimus, the faithful and dear brother, who is one of you. They will tell you about everything here.
>
> **4:10** Aristarchus, my fellow prisoner, sends you greetings, as does Mark, the cousin of Barnabas (about whom you received instructions; if he comes to you, welcome him). **4:11** And Jesus who is called Justus also sends greetings. In terms of Jewish converts, these are the only fellow workers for the kingdom of God, and they have been a comfort to me. **4:12** Epaphras, who is one of you and a slave of Christ, greets you. He is always struggling in prayer on your behalf, so that you may stand mature and fully assured in all the will of God. **4:13** For I can testify that he has worked hard for you and for those in Laodicea and Hierapolis. **4:14** Our dear friend Luke the physician and Demas greet you. **4:15** Give my greetings to the brothers and sisters who are in Laodicea and to Nympha and the church that meets in her house. **4:16** And after you have read this letter, have it read to the church of Laodicea. In turn, read the letter from Laodicea as well. **4:17** And tell Archippus, "See to it that you complete the ministry you received in the Lord." **4:18** I, Paul, write this greeting by my own hand. Remember my chains. Grace be with you.

In the book of Colossians and the book of Philemon, we find an interesting cast of characters. (In fact, I know of a seminary student who created a _Playbill_ version of Philemon, complete with actor photos. As I recall, she cast Danny DeVito as Paul, Sean Connery as Philemon, and

Demi Moore as Apphia.) Below I've listed the main characters and some of the information we have about them. Fill in what we find out in the text about each of the following individuals. (If you are a movie buff, consider whom you might cast if you were making a movie.)

2. *Apphia* (Philem. 1:2). Apphia was mostly likely Philemon's wife. How does Paul describe her?

_____

_____

_____

3. *Archippus* (Col. 4:17; Philem. 1:2). Archippus may have been Philemon and Apphia's son, or he could have been a minister in the church that met in their home. What does Paul say about him?

_____

_____

4. *Aristarchus* (Col. 4:10, 11; Philem. 1:24). Luke tells us Aristarchus was one of Paul's traveling companions from Macedonia (Acts 19:29). We find out later that Aristarchus is from the city of Thessalonica (27:2). He was one of the brothers whom the crowd dragged into the theater in Ephesus when the success of the gospel threatened the city's reputation for Artemis worship (Acts 19). How does Paul describe Aristarchus in the books of Colossians and Philemon?

_____

_____

5. *Barnabas/Joseph* (Col. 4:10, 11). Reading through the Bible, we meet Barnabas for the first time in Acts: "So Joseph, a Levite who was a native of Cyprus, called by the apostles Barnabas (which is translated 'son of encouragement'), sold a field that belonged to him and brought the money and placed it at the apostles' feet" (4:36–37). Later, when Paul became a Christian, none of the disciples wanted to

associate with him, a former Christian-killer. So Barnabas took Paul to the apostles and vouched for him. Barnabas is Paul's initial co-laborer in the gospel and is mentioned throughout the book of Acts. He is referred to here because of Mark (more on Mark later). What was Barnabas's relationship to Mark?

_____

_____

_____

6. *Demas* (Col. 4:14; Philem. 1:24). Demas's story has an unhappy ending; he deserts Paul near the end of Paul's life, having "loved this world" (2 Tim. 4:10, NIV). But when writing Colossians and Philemon, how does Paul describe him?

_____

_____

_____

7. *Epaphras* (Col. 4:12; Philem. 1:23). Paul tells the believers in Colossae, "You learned [the gospel] from Epaphras, our beloved fellow bond-servant, who is a faithful servant of Christ on our behalf, and he also informed us of your love in the Spirit" (Col. 1:7–8, NASB). Three chapters later Paul elaborates: "Epaphras, who is one of your number, a bondslave of Jesus Christ, sends you his greetings, always laboring earnestly for you in his prayers, that you may stand perfect and fully assured in all the will of God. For I bear him witness that he has a deep concern for you and for those who are in Laodicea and Hierapolis" (4:12–13, NASB). To Philemon Paul writes, "Epaphras, my fellow prisoner in Christ Jesus, sends you greetings" (Philem. 1:23). Putting it all together, it appears Epaphras was originally from Colossae and spent time in Ephesus. Once he became a transformed man, he left Ephesus to share his faith with people back at home. Many in Colossae came to know the Lord, and they formed a church full of Gentile believers. A few Jews became believers as well. Somehow Epaphras ended up in Rome and probably also imprisoned with Paul.

8. *Jesus/Justus* (Col. 4:11). What do we learn about him from this verse?

_____

_____

9. *Luke* (Col. 4:14; Philem. 1:24). Luke accompanied Paul in his travels and is credited with writing the Gospel of Luke and the book of Acts. What does Paul say about him here? What was his occupation?

_____

_____

_____

10. *Mark* (Col. 4:10, 11; Philem. 1:24). Barnabas's cousin. Also called John or John Mark, Mark traveled with Barnabas and Paul, who worked as an evangelistic team sharing the good news of Jesus Christ. The believers were meeting at Mark's mother's house in Jerusalem when Peter was released from prison by an angel (Acts 12).

Paul and Barnabas faced many hardships as they ministered, and when they reached Pamphylia, John Mark decided he didn't want to go further with them, so he returned to Jerusalem (Acts 13:13). Later, Barnabas wanted to include John Mark on another missionary journey, but Paul said no because John Mark had deserted them earlier (Acts 15:37–39). The disagreement between Paul and Barnabas was so sharp that they went their separate ways—Barnabas taking Mark and Paul teaming up with Silas. If Paul is now asking the church at Colossae to welcome Mark, what does that say about his opinion of Mark some years after the disagreement?

_____

_____

_____

At the end of his life, Paul writes to Timothy, "Only Luke is with me. Pick up Mark and bring him with you, for he is useful to me for service. But Tychicus I have sent to Ephesus" (2 Tim 4:11–12, NASB).

11. *Nympha* (Col. 4:15). What do we learn about Nympha from this text?

_____

_____

_____

12. *Onesimus* (Col. 4:9, 11; Philem. 1:10–16). Onesimus is the former slave of Philemon. His name means "useful," so Paul does a play on words with *useful* and *useless* in Philemon 1:11. Approximately one-half to one-third of those in the Roman Empire were slaves—an estimated sixty million people. Roman slavery was not based on race; many slaves were prisoners of war and the crème de la crème of society, including doctors, lawyers, and teachers who practiced their professions in bondage. Paul describes Onesimus as "our faithful and beloved brother, who is one of your number" (Col. 4:9, NASB). Some believe Onesimus stole money[11] from Philemon (because Paul wrote, "If he owes you anything, charge it to my account" in Philemon 1:18)—a crime punishable by death. Rebellious slaves, if not put to death, were branded on the forehead with an *F* (*fugitivus* or "fugitive") or *CF* (*cave furem*, "beware of thief").[12] Whether he was a thief, Onesimus had run away from his master in Colossae and had somehow connected with Paul, probably in Rome. There Paul led him to the Lord, grounded him in the faith, and sent him back to his master accompanied by Tychicus. (Slaves in the Roman Empire had no legal rights; they were considered property. Eventually they were granted protective legislation comparable to our animal-rights laws.[13]) Church history records that Onesimus was eventually martyred (see footnote on p. xi).

Paul wants to keep Onesimus with him, but Onesimus needs to go back, risking his life, to make amends with Philemon. Paul sends with

[11] *Eerdmans' Handbook to the Bible*, 625.
[12] Kent Hughes, *Colossians and Philemon: The Supremacy of Christ* (Colorado Springs: NavPress), 161.
[13] Hughes, 122.

Onesimus his good friend Tychicus and a letter to the Colossians and to Philemon. In the short missive to Philemon, he asks his friend to go easy on the slave, appealing to providence: "Perhaps he was for this reason separated from you for a while, that you would have him back forever" (Philem. 1:15, NASB). What does this say about providence? And what does it say about the need to make restitution?

---

13. *Paul* (Col. 1:1; Philem. 1:1). Paul's background is included in the introduction to this study.

14. *Philemon* (Philem. 1:1). The name means "affectionate." Philemon lives in Colossae, where tradition says he was bishop, and that he was eventually martyred.[14] Philemon is one of Paul's converts: "You owe to me your very self" (Philem.1:19). Paul says of him, "I have come to have much joy and comfort in your love, because the hearts of the saints have been refreshed through you, brother" (1:7, NASB). Philemon is apparently a man of enough means to own a slave, and as a master he probably held life-and-death power over his human property.

15. *Timothy* (Col. 1:1; Philem. 1:1). Acts 16:1 tells us that Timothy, from the town of Derbe,[15] was the son of a Jewish mother and a Greek father. Both his mother and grandmother were women of faith (2 Tim. 1:5). He is Paul's "son in the Lord" (1 Cor. 4:17), and two of Paul's epistles—the books of 1 and 2 Timothy—are addressed to him, providing pastoral instructions. What do we learn about Timothy from the references in Colossians and Philemon?

---

[14] *Unger's Bible Dictionary,* 856.
[15] Or perhaps Lystra. See Acts 14:6, 16:1 and 20:4.

16. *Tychicus* (Col. 4:7–9, 11). Tychicus returned to Colossae with Onesimus from Rome when Onesimus returned to his master. According to Acts 20:4, Tychicus was from Asia, and he traveled some with Paul and on his behalf. Paul writes in Colossians 4:7, "As to all my affairs, Tychicus, our beloved brother and faithful servant and fellow bond-servant in the Lord, will bring you information" (NASB). Tychicus probably witnessed the great Ephesian riot that prompted Paul to depart Ephesus for Macedonia (Acts 19:34–20:1) and if so, he would have experienced danger himself and shared Paul's bravery. Over in Ephesians 6:21, Paul writes, "About my circumstances, how I am doing, Tychicus, the beloved brother and faithful minister in the Lord, will make everything known to you" (NASB). To Titus, Paul writes, "When I send Artemas or Tychicus to you, make every effort to come to me at Nicopolis, for I have decided to spend the winter there" (Titus 3:12, NASB). At the end of Paul's life, he writes to Timothy, "Only Luke is with me. Pick up Mark and bring him with you, for he is useful to me for service. But Tychicus I have sent to Ephesus" (2 Tim. 4:11–12, NASB). So throughout Paul's life we see Tychicus traveling on the apostle's behalf. Tychicus is not noted for his gifts, which were surely many or he would not have been given so much responsibility. Rather, he is constantly mentioned as serving Paul in the ministry of the gospel. How does Paul describe him in the book of Colossians?

_____

_____

_____

17. By looking at all these mini biographies, we can make some observations: Paul ministered in the context of community; he did not try to do it all by himself, talented as he was. He delegated many tasks, and he mentored many in the faith.

With whom are you partnering in the exercise of your spiritual gift?

_____

_____

Whose life are you helping to develop with eternal instruction? If no one, whom could you start mentoring?

_____

_____

_____

*"I, Paul, write this greeting by my own hand"* (Col 4:18). As we mentioned in the introduction to this study, Paul probably had an *amanuensis*—a secretary—to whom he dictated his letters. Tychicus may have served in this capacity and then delivered the letters. Some think Paul's "thorn in the flesh" (2 Cor. 12:7) was poor eyesight, possibly a lasting effect from his blindness on the road to Damascus (Acts 9:3). Such a malady would have required him to use help when drafting a lengthy document. Consider that to the Galatians he writes, "See what big letters I make as I write to you with my own hand!" (Gal. 6:11).

Whether he used a secretary out of need or convenience, we know Paul sometimes used one. At the end of the book of Romans, we read, "I, Tertius, who wrote down this letter, greet you in the Lord" (Rom. 16:22). And notice that Colossians 4:18 says Paul is writing the "greeting" and not the "letter" with his own hand. In Philemon 1:19, Paul says he is writing the letter with his own hand in the middle of the section where he tells Philemon to charge any of Onesimus's debts to him. The epistle to Philemon may have been so personal and so short that he elected to write it himself.

• *Remember my chains.* Whether Paul means these words (Col. 4:18) as a prayer request or a reminder of the cost he has paid and is paying for taking the gospel to the Gentiles, we get a glimpse of the discomfort he experiences as he writes. He has no assurance that he will ever again be free or if he'll be spared execution when his case finally comes to Caesar's court. Of this short phrase, the late Ray Stedman said,

> Paul himself has been in glory all these centuries, and yet these words still have meaning for us. It is well for us too to remember his chains, to think of this mighty apostle who was hounded, persecuted and oppressed everywhere he went. He was resisted and thrown into jail in many places. He spent a

night and a day in the deep. He was beaten with rods and stoned on occasion. Even as he writes these letters he does not find it easy to do so. He does not sit down in a comfortable room with his word processor. He must dictate them to an educated slave, and then painfully, because he suffered from poor eyesight, write with large letters his name at the close, lest the letter be treated as a forgery. Down through the centuries this letter, along with others, has transformed the history of the world. It is a tremendously important document. Yet it is well for us to remember the cost of having these scriptures in our own hands. 'Remember my chains.' Let us give thanks for this apostle who kept the Lord always at the center of his thoughts. Heedless of obstacles, he fulfilled his own ministry faithfully before the Lord. What a model he is to us![16]

• *Grace be with you.* Paul ends his epistle the same way he began, with a salutation of grace to his readers. Grace is the core message of Paul's ministry, and grace is what sets Christianity apart from every other religion. In Paul's own words on the subject, "By grace you are saved through faith, and this is not from yourselves, it is the gift of God; it is not from works, so that no one can boast" (Eph. 2:8–9).

---

[16] Ray Stedman, "Expository Studies in Colossians: The Early-Day Saints," 1986 (www.raystedman.org/colossians, accessed December 29, 2006)

1. In the history of the nation of Israel, God gave some specific instructions to Moses, which he recorded in what is now the book of Deuteronomy in the Bible. One command included what the king was to do with God's law:

> When you come to the land the Lord your God is giving you and take it over and live in it and then say, "I will select a king like all the nations surrounding me," you must select without fail a king whom the Lord your God chooses. . . . When he sits on his royal throne he must make a copy of this law on a scroll given to him by the Levitical priests. It must be with him constantly and he must read it as long as he lives, so that he may learn to revere the Lord his God and observe all the words of this law and these statutes and carry them out. Then he will not exalt himself above his fellow citizens or turn from the commandments to the right or left, and he and his descendants will enjoy many years ruling over his kingdom in Israel (Deut. 17:14–15; 18–20).

One of my mentors suggested that I purchase a lined journal and do as the king did—write out the entire book of Deuteronomy. That was no small task! It took about a year of Sundays, in one- or two-hour segments, to do so, but I finally finished. The beauty of the assignment was that it forced me—in this blow-your-hair-back world of speeding from one task to another—to slow down and chew on every letter in the text. I was astounded at the holiness of God as I paid close attention to the blessings and curses promised to Israel, depending on whether they obeyed. I noticed details I had glossed over in other readings too. Odd names stuck out. Repeated locations took on complex histories as I connected what God did in a town and then returned to do later—and again even later—in the same place.

When I was in college, my Pauline Epistles professor assigned a similar project. Each time we studied a book—whether medium-length Galatians or even the lengthy Book of Acts—he had us write out the book in longhand. First we charted main ideas in big boxes for outlines. Then we filled in every word from the text. We used colored pencils to highlight repeated words and phrases and meditated on the thoughts as we copied the words. I grew to appreciate how easy it would have been for a scribe to miss a letter or even an entire line, especially when two lines started with the same word.

Now it's your turn. Spend the next two days writing out the book of Colossians in your own notebook. As you do, chew on Paul's words. Notice how he exalts Christ. Think about how important it was to Paul to spread the inclusive gospel to the Gentiles. Pray with him the great prayer offered on behalf of the Colossian believers—only this time fill in your own name and the names of those you love.

Such slow interaction with God's Word is more than an antidote to protect us from the poison of fast times. It's a form of meditation that comes with the rewards promised in Psalm 1. The person who meditates on God's Word is "like a tree firmly planted by streams of water, which yields its fruit in its season" (NASB). And remember? That's likely the image Paul had in mind when he told the Colossians to be "rooted and built up in him and firm in your faith just as you were taught, and overflowing with thankfulness" (2:7).

Even though the chapter and verse numbers are included, I recommend leaving them out so you get the sense of how the letter flowed without interruption. Now, pray for insight and write Colossians 1 and 2.

2. What stood out to you as you copied from Colossians today?

_____

_____

3. What blessed you as you wrote?

_____

_____

## FRIDAY: THE SECOND HALF

1. Pray for insight from the Spirit; then continue writing out the rest of Colossians. When you're finished, answer today's questions.

2. Now that you're finished writing, what did you observe? Any words repeated? Concepts emphasized?

_____

_____

_____

_____

3. What stood out to you as particularly meaningful?

_____

_____

4. Were you convicted by a particular command or example you need to follow? If so, what?

_____

_____

## SATURDAY: FALLING INTO THE ARMS OF LOVE

**Scripture:** "Therefore, as the elect of God, holy and dearly loved, clothe yourselves with a heart of mercy, kindness, humility, gentleness, and patience, bearing with one another and forgiving one another, if someone happens to have a complaint against anyone else. Just as the Lord has forgiven you, so you also forgive others. And to all these virtues add love, which is the perfect bond." (Colossians 3:12–14)

It happened in an instant, yet it took a long time as instants go. I felt it all in slow motion. One moment I stood in heels at the top of the steps; the next, I tumbled down headfirst. To keep from slamming my noggin into the wall at the end of the landing, I ducked. And I broke my collarbone. Banged up my shoulder. Fractured a couple of ribs.

It's not that I failed to hold on. I had my hand on the rail. But my heel caught in the carpet, and my computer bag, slung over my left shoulder, lunged forward when I tripped. I might have recovered my balance had it not been for that heavy load yanking me forward, cooperating with gravity to slam me down.

Our daughter was playing in the backyard. Usually at 5:10 PM, the time it happened, she and I have the place to ourselves. Any other day I would have been inside alone, but my mother-in-law, who had come to help with homework, was still there, sitting at the kitchen table reading. She heard me scream and dashed to my rescue.

I couldn't get up on my own.

My husband usually arrives home around six, but he had left the office a little early to get here in time to care for our daughter so I could drive into town and deliver a ninety-minute lecture on bioethics. (You can bet that didn't happen.) When I called him, he was about ten minutes from home. When he arrived, I took one look at his face and fell in love all over again.

"Where do you want me to take you?" he asked, as if plotting a dinner date.

"Baylor Hospital. Downtown."

"It takes longer to get there. Why not the local one?"

The place that misdiagnosed our daughter's broken elbow? Not a chance.

He drove me to Dallas's Baylor ER while Grammy cared for our daughter. I could feel the break. But what evoked my real fear was the pain when I exhaled. I hoped I hadn't punctured a lung. The thirty-minute drive, filled with tears, moans on every exhale, and prayers for mercy felt like it took a month.

Then we walked into the ER and found a crowd of about thirty people ahead of us. Desperation set in. I imagined myself sitting there for three hours. Please, no!

The triage nurse asked what happened. I told her I'd fallen down the steps. To my amazement, she looked me in the eye and said, "I'm so sorry," before going on to ask my name and insurance coverage. I was a person, not a case, not a shoulder injury, not a potential punctured lung. Nothing makes me want to bawl like a little empathy.

*"Keep it together, keep it together."* I mentally repeated Eddie Murphy's lines from *Bowfinger*.

The nurses took one look at me all wobbly, breathing fast, moaning, with my right shoulder a full inch higher than my left (they even said so aloud!), and ushered me right into a room. Then I didn't know if I should rejoice that I got to the head of the line or despair that whatever was wrong looked serious.

But I needn't have confused getting a room with getting attention. Silly me. Still, it beat waiting out in the lobby.

Over the course of the next six hours, they shot mobile x-rays of my collar bone (broken royally—snapped in two) and took x-rays of my chest and drew blood for some tests to make sure I was up for a CT scan, which I was. So I drank the syrupy, grape-flavored metal stuff designed to light up my innards for the machine. (Gag me with a forklift.)

The nurse led me in for the scan. The tech shot some pictures and then put iodine in my IV, and I felt like I was heating up from the core out. Once the medical team gave me the all-clear in the absence of internal bleeding, they pumped me full of painkillers (finally!) and gave me something to make me loopy. (As if I needed help.)

They recommended rest. Lots of rest and meds for the pain. And a year and two surgeries later—including bone grafts off the hip—I'm still on the mend. That's the medical side.

But it gets better. Seriously.

The men's Bible study, meeting at the church building when my husband called from the ER, headed on down to hang out with us. The prayer chain sent out e-mail messages. People really prayed.

When we called home from the ER at 9 that night to say we'd be a while, Grammy said, "Your daughter is in bed already, and I'm lying next to her on her floor." I didn't have time to stop and ponder such grandparently love before she added, "She says to tell Mommy she loves you and that the kitties send their love too."

Wow, the cats love me. Who knew?

The next day my sis called to say I could match the purple girl in *Willy Wonka and the Chocolate Factory*. (She always provides the warped sort of comfort that would leave other people aghast but which I am twisted enough to appreciate.)

By 2 PM a meal arrived—the first of six weeks' worth that continued well after we told everybody to stop bringing food. The tech at my doctor's office marveled at how we were cared for. People sent e-mails. Some added silly photo attachments to cheer me. Others phoned. My niece baked me a cake. Dallas Seminary's chaplain called, and his prayer made me laugh and cry—laugh because he prayed that such things are supposed to happen only to old women; cry because through his words I felt the presence and tender love of God.

The church is Christ's body—His arms hugging and feeding and loving. Our brothers and sisters loved us well, showing up as "Jesus with skin on." Yes, I took a nasty fall—right into the arms of love.

Paul wrote to the Colossians, "Therefore, as God's chosen people, holy and dearly loved, clothe yourselves with compassion, kindness, humility, gentleness and patience. Bear with each other. . . . And over all these virtues put on love, which binds them all together in perfect unity" (Colossians 3:12–14, NIV). The ultimate witness to the world is how members of the body of Christ love one another. When I fell, I experienced once again that kind of love—the kind of love that can't be repaid.

It's breathtaking.

And, frankly, why shouldn't we love like that—all dressed up in Christlikeness? The Creator and sustainer of the universe took on human flesh and met our need when we were too helpless to do anything for ourselves. We should never get over the gratitude.

Have you trusted in His perfect sacrifice? If so, have you changed your wardrobe?

**Prayer:** *Lord Christ, You are the image of the invisible God, the first-born of all creation. By You all things were created in heaven and earth, visible and invisible, whether thrones or dominions or rulers or authorities, all things were created by You and for You. Thank You for Your magnificence in nature. Thank You that You are all-powerful. Thank You that You have the power to change me. I, too, am your creation—made by You and for You. Through the power of the Holy Spirit, grant me the ability to know fully who I am and to put off the old person with its fleshly attachments, the anger, the selfishness. Clothe me, instead, in the compassion, humility, gentleness, patience, and love that's becoming to Your creation. Grant me, because of Your grace, to treat everyone as a member of Your beloved creation, with dignity and honor. Be exalted through my life. Help me to walk worthy of the great calling I have through Your finished work on the Cross. In my own imperfect way, I love You, Lord. Help me to mature in You, to grow deeper, to bear the fruit of a godly life. Help me to trust You through difficulty. And use me to spread the good news of Your great holiness and love. I ask these things in Your name, Amen.*

**For Memorization:** "Conduct yourselves with wisdom toward outsiders, making the most of the opportunities. Let your speech always be gracious, seasoned with salt, so that you may know how you should answer everyone.